Vintage vavoom

ROMANTIC DECORATING WITH ONE-OF-A-KIND FINDS

The Editors of **ROMANTIC HOMES** *Magazine* | *Romantic* HOMES

CLARKSON POTTER/PUBLISHERS

NEW YORK

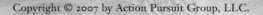

Copyright © 2007 by Action Pursuit Group, LLC.

All rights reserved.
Published in the United States by Clarkson Potter/Publishers,
an imprint of the Crown Publishing Group,
a division of Random House, Inc., New York.
www.crownpublishing.com
www.clarksonpotter.com

Library of Congress Cataloging-in-Publication Data
Vintage vavoom : romantic decorating with one-of-a-kind
finds / the editors of Romantic Homes magazine. — 1st ed.
    Includes index.
    1. Antiques in interior decoration.
    2. Interior decoration—Psychological aspects.
I. Romantic homes.   II. Title.
NK2115.5.A5.V56   2007
747—dc22   2007006761

ISBN 978-0-307-38274-0

Printed in China

Design by Laura Palese

10 9 8 7 6 5 4 3 2 1

First Edition

CONTENTS

INTRODUCTION

What is Vintage Vavoom?

Vintage Vavoom is a style that combines the best decorative looks of the past with the sensibilities and passions of today. It is a style that prizes pieces with a romantic history, but nonetheless transcends trends and time.

Whether inspired by fond remembrances of the house you grew up in, heirlooms lovingly handed down, or the décor of a home you always aspired to live in, Vintage Vavoom is personal yet universally appealing.

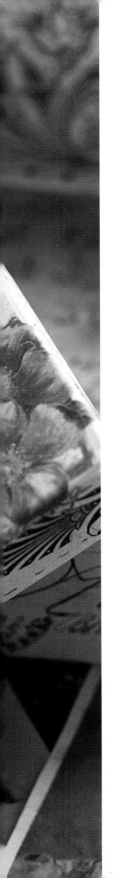

A HOME SHOULD NOT BE A TIME CAPSULE FROM AN ERA WHEN calling cards were delivered on silver trays. Naturally, we are charmed by customs that could be cribbed from an Edith Wharton novel; however, that kind of formality isn't suitable for today's living. Instead, we create a classic look for today by combining favored items from the past with newer pieces and design trends.

Take color, for example. In past years, we've seen a revolving palette of haute colors, from turquoise and coral to pink and brown. Using such colorful schemes in your rooms is a quick, whimsical way to add flair. Displays are also a form of expressing Vintage Vavoom. In this book, we share examples of how showcasing collections, everyday items, and even a three-tiered bounty of fruit become thoughtful strokes on a captivating canvas.

Creating a home built around comfort and beauty is a personal exercise. Vintage Vavoom is distinctive in that no two pieces or groupings are alike. It's the quality found in a house with a story behind every piece, a place inhabited by homeowners who gave up restricting pets from the couch and found charm in seeing the family dog's hair magnetized to an heirloom blanket. It's the music of creaky floors, the clamor of mismatched china, and the marriage of two generations of silver that somehow dazzle in one brilliant symphony. It's the handmade damask pillow bought from the antiques dealer who sat behind the old cash register with a bell on it.

"Decorate by following your instincts. Marry things you love, and they will relate to one another."

Create your own special memory box for precious heirlooms and mementos you intend to pass down to future generations.

Now the Day So sweetly Closes.

In the following chapters, we show you how to create Vintage Vavoom with heirlooms; pieces acquired from trips, flea markets, or consignment shops; and treasures won on eBay. You'll also learn to find inspiration in everything colorful and modern yet rooted in tradition—a good tradition, one that's not about gimmicks.

What groovy is to the coffee table made from a surfboard, Vintage Vavoom is to your mother's wedding china gleaming in a glass-fronted cabinet. We can connect opposing things through the magic of color and light. A well-dressed dessert is spiffed up with the right cake plate. While one heavy linen tea towel is certainly pretty, grouped in a stack with similar pieces, it's a knockout. Think silver teapots filled with calla lilies, eye-catching fabric remnants piled in a rattan basket, patina-blue ceramics enlivening a cupboard with a rickety door, and old family photographs displayed in creative ways.

LEFT: One of the trademarks of Vintage Vavoom is an assortment of vintage linen.

OPPOSITE, ABOVE: A grouping of one-of-a-kind finds that share vintage texture, color, and classic detailing has true Vintage Vavoom style.

Chances are a person who lives in a romantic home with Vintage Vavoom can tolerate the evening rush-hour traffic with soothing thoughts of that big squashy chair with the petal-soft pillow waiting to welcome her home. She can easily imagine stepping through the door into rooms that call for cotton night-gowns and a cup of tea—the kind made with loose leaves—where the only disruption is the whistling of the kettle. The notes of this décor are lush colors, treasures culled from shopping expeditions, layers of sumptuous textiles, the scent of flowers and candles. While Vintage Vavoom pieces can be functional and undoubt-edly beautiful, they may also be guiltlessly acquired for the sake of pure indulgence, like escaping to a matinée when you have a week's worth of laundry to do.

Nowadays, we see all too many McMansions loaded with gadgets that can be operated only if you're willing to read a hundred-page manual. These elements are as inspiring as a cereal label. Homes with Vintage Vavoom

TOP: You can find beauty in the simplest of items, such as the rolls of ribbons that comple-ment the rose pat-tern of this bud vase.

ABOVE: Versatile, multicolored fabrics can be found at flea markets for a song. Start a collection to add a colorful mix to your more subdued pieces.

RIGHT: Textiles are just one simple way to add color to your room.

BELOW: Adding a jolt of color to your home is as simple as displaying brightly colored produce in a favored pedestal bowl.

OPPOSITE, LEFT: Be inspired by your favorite shops, where store owners find innovative ideas in lovely pieces.

OPPOSITE, RIGHT: Liberate favored pieces to add glamour in everyday living.

style can include all the best features of today—and we show you how these rooms can possess all the romance of a mysterious love letter. This is a book you will spend time with and tuck away just before falling under the spell of sleep. You may even find it inspires your nighttime reveries!

Decorate by following your instincts. Marry things you love, and they will relate to one another. The Vintage Vavoom home says, "Be with me; let's play, break the rules, and be happy together." Showing such confidence in your decorating approach may be the most important criterion of all.

Throughout the pages of this book, we share ideas and concepts to help you create your personal brand of Vintage Vavoom. Keep in mind these dominant themes:

§ Combine vintage and newer pieces to achieve that special lived-in feeling.

§ Weave Vintage Vavoom pieces into your rooms for a one-of-a-kind home that combines beauty and personality.

§ If you love something, there is a place for it in your home. Follow your passions, whether displaying heirloom pieces connecting you to your childhood or a love for cooking, and translate them into your surroundings.

§ Look to the past while honoring your current sensibilities.

§ If you find a piece that makes you gush, consider it an investment. When you have to scratch the itch to give in to a trend, save your money by buying a few well-chosen and affordable mass-produced items.

§ Find inspiration from people or places that reflect your sensibilities, such as your favorite shopkeeper's displays or an antiques market.

§ Go on a treasure hunt to find unique pieces that will give you that feel-good lift when added to your home.

§ Be confident! Decorate to your taste, and personalization happens.

§ Imperfection is not only a refreshing break from the matchy-matchy, just-off-the-production-cycle look; it's a sign of character that adds beauty.

§ Flowers, fruit, food, and natural elements add instant zing to a room.

§ Liberate forgotten treasures to add interest to any vignette.

Vintage Vavoom
DREAM DIARY WORKSHOP

At the end of each chapter, you'll attend a Vintage Vavoom Workshop to help you get your ideas and preferences out of your head and onto paper. Just as professional designers compile resources to spark their inspiration before beginning a project, you will use the same tools to start mapping your own individual décor dreamscape.

Everything from fabrics, textures, and color chips to floor plans, photos, and simple sketches can be included in your personal record. You might include a picture of a throw pillow you'd like to sew on one page, and an article on a kitchen makeover you've fallen in love with on the next. By the end, you will have created a unique, tailor-made home décor map that reflects who you are now—and where you strive to go. You're encouraged to start with an open mind, without pre-conceived notions and without judging as you go along. Don't worry about how you'll realize these dreams—getting them down in your notebook is the first step. You don't know where this road will lead you until you've reached the end. There may be some surprises! Once your notebook is completed, you will always have this inspirational tool handy for reference when making decisions on the next home project you tackle.

GETTING STARTED:
Make Your Workbook

Materials:

One 2-inch, three-ring, loose-leaf binder

Notebook paper, lined and unlined

Binder dividers (make your own or purchase ready-made)

Labels for dividers

Pens, pencils, crayons, etc.

Scissors

Three-hole punch

Top-loading clear plastic sheet protectors

Magazines, copies of favorite photos, color chips, fabric swatches, etc., for inspiration, information, and collages

Optional: fabric, paper, stickers, labels, or other decorations to cover or embellish a plain binder

Preparing Your Dream Diary

If you purchase a plain binder, you may want to decorate it or label it to make it your own. Or, purchase a decorative binder that you love. Either way, make sure you have a binder that "sings" to you; it will be much more fun to reach for as you compile your Vintage Vavoom Dream Diary.

Next, make the following section labels:

1. Bringing in the Vavoom
2. Quality Counts
3. Shopping
4. Color
5. Mix and Match
6. Displays of Affection
7. Personalized Style
8. Basics of Care
9. My Dream Home—Interior
   a. Kitchen
   b. Bath
   c. Bedrooms (you may want to break this down into Master, Children's, Guest)
   d. Dining Room
   e. Living/Family Room
   f. Other
10. My Dream Home—Exterior
    a. Home Style
    b. Garden
    c. Other
11. Resources
12. Miscellaneous

Put the sections of your binder together and add some plain and lined paper to each, as well as a few of the sheet protectors. You may need only lined paper in the Resources section, although some of us like to collect business cards. Now, with your workbook binder organized and tools at the ready, you'll begin compiling your Vintage Vavoom Dream Diary with the next chapter's workshop installment.

1

BRINGING IN THE VAVOOM

Creating the Look

The etymology of "vavoom" dates to 1969, a time when the sweet but swanky girl next door turned heads with a new confidence as she marched into the Summer of Love.

We all know the look—that special sense of style that draws you in. In showing the world her personal flair, she allowed you to learn something about her that left you craving to know more. A home can have the same appeal, which we've defined as Vintage Vavoom. Its whimsy, elegance, intelligence, and sense of history pique your interest. The home's distinct style expresses volumes about the person who created it.

LIKE THE WARM KITCHEN YOU GREW UP IN, NOSTALGIA IS AT THE HEART of this style. Vintage décor, with thoughtful planning and a fresh, modern sensibility, can attract your attention and say, "Come in; put your feet up and stay awhile." Translate this kind of warmth and invitation into your rooms with mismatched china stacked in crooked heaps, punctuated with Caribbean blue vases here and there. In Bountiful, Sue Balmforth's Venice, California, shop, there is a happy mix of shiny and worn, soft and hard, functional and purely, unabashedly decorative. The rules are loose, says Balmforth: Put together pieces you find irresistible.

PRECEDING PAGE: Find soft, romantic touches in distressed pieces, flowers, and a sparkly chandelier.

ABOVE LEFT: It takes very little to create Vintage Vavoom; gently distressed furniture, fresh flowers, and family photographs in vintage frames are just a few of the basics.

ABOVE RIGHT: An antique perfume shop display case is the perfect place for a favorite vignette.

OPPOSITE: Open shelving at the Venice, California, shop Bountiful sets a retro tone.

This inviting look will inspire you to turn off the big-screen television and bring back the timeless tradition of entertaining guests who linger well into the night over good conversation, bellies happily filled with delicious food and so much laughter it floats freely into the night sky. By following a few basic principles, you can inject Vintage Vavoom into your own home. Begin by discovering your personal style, and you'll soon see how to take the basic elements in your home to the next level—like adding chocolate syrup and sprinkles to a bowl of vanilla ice cream. It may seem paradoxical, but it is actually the details that establish the foundation of your look. Details that show a distinct style express personality. Achieve your own, distinctive variety of Vintage Vavoom with these tips:

TOP: These plump pillows, covered in soft blue French fabric, say cottage chic with flair.

ABOVE: At Bountiful, natural light adds sparkle to favorite collectibles, while fresh flowers add elegance.

A classic fabric pattern trimmed with simple tassles adds drama to a porch corner.

Elegant his-and-hers towels are a fun display in the guest bathroom.

THE PRINCIPLES OF VINTAGE VAVOOM

- *Feature unique pieces (one-of-a-kind decorative details such as heirlooms, china patterns, etc.).*

- *Choose items that are timeless and well made.*

- *Create a layered look.*

- *Decorate with care and thoughtful consideration of how elements play off each other.*

- *Imbue your home with a sense of history and nostalgia.*

- *Emphasize a soft, romantic look.*

- *Mix the old with the new.*

- *Personalize your living space.*

- *Keep affordability in mind.*

- *Give your possessions unconditional love.*

Unique Pieces

Take a walk around your home and pay particular attention to those accent pieces that most clearly express your room's feel. You will notice that you have enlisted a variety of items to compose your home's look. The pieces may have a particular color or shape that you are drawn to. Perhaps many of them were manufactured in a particular period or region. These special pieces are the foundation of your home's unique style.

Timeless, Well-Made Items

Elegance abounds in the perfect curve of a dressing table leg that is unmistakably French. To get Vintage Vavoom, visit the classics. More than an ocean separates us from Europe when it comes to a household item's expiration date. European designs have a long and venerable history to draw

OPPOSITE: Vintage perfume bottles add sparkle and a feminine touch when displayed on a mantel.

LEFT: Often, finding china and crystal pieces, such as this Victorian-style wash bowl, teacup, and trio of candlesticks, is a mere matter of scouring garage sales and flea markets.

upon, and Europeans are less inclined to purge a house of its longtime belongings in favor of the "new and improved" models many Americans prefer. Consider Americana a respected contributor to the Vintage Vavoom mix too, though. Seek out fantastic items like the sturdy basic milk stool weathered by generations of Amish bottoms or the retro doo-wop tableware once used to serve a strawberry shake with two straws at a diner. The definition of *classic* has expanded to include those items done well, pieces that express a style to an admiring clientele. One essential aspect of the Vintage Vavoom spirit is how something is produced. (We explore this and train your eye in Chapter 2, "Quality Counts.") Anything hand-painted or lovingly crafted has this spirit, which increases its qualitative value. For instance, is the piece

Cute, collectible, and providing a timeless function, vintage baking pieces add instant flavor to a kitchen.

OPPOSITE: A simple sheer around a bathtub can infuse a bathroom with romance.

RIGHT: Shells make for great design touches. Showcase them in a candy dish, glue them to candlestick holders and frames, or situate them in any empty space.

handcrafted or machine-made? Assess the quality of the materials used, the ornamentation, and the overall substance. If something has endured for decades, it was made well. If a newer piece is made with care, with thoughtful preservation it can be a future heirloom.

A Layered Look

Have fun mixing design styles and different pieces. Keep in mind that it's important to link common traits when composing your home's décor so it does not appear overly decorated or cluttered. (You'll find more on this in Chapter 5, "Mix and Match.") Consider decorative movements. There is a variety to choose from, such as Scandinavian, Victoriana, French country, shabby chic, and beach cottage. In your own home, look to such themes for inspiration while mixing in things you already own and cherish. Family heirlooms always add interest to a grouping, but you can also enhance its richness by featuring

everyday items like that collection of animated pie birds you actually use. Household items with creative packaging and elements from Mother Nature offer expressions of timelessness that can fuel your decorating muse. Shells you collected from a beach holiday have more impact in a crystal candy dish than a bag of saltwater taffy bought at the airport newsstand.

Thoughtful Consideration

One common pitfall decorators stumble into is the idea that they need to decorate with everything they own. Perhaps it's the guilt of not giving a piece its due moment, to be showcased and admired. However, like the tired star athlete who needs bench time for refreshment, our items maintain their shine if we give them necessary time out of rotation.

Part of the fun of decorating is changing things around—a perfect opportunity to evaluate those stored pieces to see if they will add to a new look. Just as a shopkeeper has to keep displays fresh, update your vignettes. Take another tip from the pros and create your own prop closet to rotate your treasures. By giving your favored treasures their own space, you can easily revisit them when you are struck by a decorating whim.

Before indulging an urge to purchase something new, consider what you own. Chances are you have many versions of the same thing. The savings are not only in storage and cost; repurposing things you already own doesn't strain the world's resources. Environmentalists take note: Vintage Vavoom is very much about green living. A pure form of decorating is to reuse not just what you own but what has been used by others in centuries past.

"Part of the fun of decorating is changing things around—a perfect opportunity to evaluate those stored pieces to see if they will add to a new look."

Hanging a chandelier in an unexpected place, refurbishing heirloom pieces with fresh paint, and sprinkling in roses opening to a second-day bloom heighten a room's golly-gee factor. The personality is inviting and easy to live with, while you are the definite author of the look.

A charming paint-chipped mirror reflects roses and light while doubling as a diminutive tray.

shopping list

Where can you find Vintage Vavoom? If something was beloved and used in your family for generations, it has Vintage Vavoom. Want to shop for items? Browse for the following:

- Heirloom china and silverware
- Tiaras
- Vintage hotel dinnerware
- Colorful plates to use as wall hangings
- Pie birds
- Vintage salt and pepper shakers
- Apothecary jars filled with textured items— from old buttons to colorful ribbons
- Old timepieces (not the falsely aged ones)
- Tea towels
- Antique tablecloths
- Crocheted cocktail napkins
- Lacy pillowcases
- Metal lunch boxes that remind you of the one you brought with you to your first day of second grade
- Chandeliers
- Used books
- Wire baskets
- Vintage photographs
- Garden ornaments, such as finials, old tools, trellises, and urns
- Cracked mirrors (Someone's bad luck can be your good fortune!)
- Weathered signs
- Metal frogs
- Ironstone pieces
- Kitchen collectibles

- Shells, starfish, and beach art, such as old lithographs of shells
- Mirrored boxes and picture frames
- Perfume bottles
- Architectural salvage, such as columns and stained-glass windows
- Cabinet hardware
- Typesetting hardware
- Old playing cards and games
- Strands of pearls (real or fake)
- Feather boas, the kind a flapper would have worn
- Bolts of fabric
- Old keys
- Postcards from another time
- Handcrafted soaps and bath items
- Cut crystal vases
- Old hatboxes
- Ornamental slippers
- Colorful feathers
- Vintage fans
- China dolls
- Cake plates
- Vintage tea canisters

In the next chapters, you'll learn all about how to shop for vintage and how to spot one-of-a-kind, high-quality finds.

PRECEDING PAGE: Fine china with intricate patterns is a staple of the Vintage Vavoom look.

LEFT: Jeweled theatrical crowns and tiaras complement the china and express the glamour of days gone by.

Vintage Vavoom is not the young girl dressed in a mishmash of thrift-store clothes, text messaging her friend across the room, nor is it the fussy lady who lunches loaded with jewelry, fumigating her space with heavy perfume. It's the woman who has a classic style but is gutsy enough to bring in the textured yet soft details that distinguish her own look. She sets the table with matching china carefully chosen during the rituals of her engagement, and then brings in those little ice-cream-parlor glasses she used and loved when she lived in her first apartment.

Comfortable, Not Cluttered

The guiding principle in creating a comfortable home is decorating with what you love but being careful not to overdo it. Vintage Vavoom is not a cluttered look. To show off your found items, focus on a few key areas in your home and style thoughtful, attractive arrangements rather than showcase everything you own, which is so Ivana Trump circa 1986. Consider how the pieces relate to one another by means of a shared texture, color, or theme. (See Chapter 5, "Mix and Match.")

LEFT: A French toile wallpaper backdrop adds vavoom to this setting of treasured vintage medicine jars and a dressed-up refurbished lamp.

OPPOSITE: The variety of patterns and shapes of these antique pieces is fun yet elegant.

ABOVE: Your best china isn't fussy when paired with sugar cubes mixed with jelly beans.

RIGHT: A rose wrapped in baby bok choy leaves, with an egg cup as the chosen vessel, distinguishes this setting.

LEFT: Pink carnations are a cheerful hallmark of Vintage Vavoom cottage elegance.

BELOW: Vintage china is a timeless decorating staple that blends easily with your other collectibles.

History and Nostalgia

One-of-a-kind pieces are irreplaceable; how-ever, the prune jar with the embossed mea-surements your mother used for baking also has value. Consider the unlikely pieces that can make you smile or bring you comfort. Of course, beauty factors into a piece's worth, but so do whimsy and rich subtext.

Often we are drawn to the things we grew up with. Tea tastes better in the cups your grand-mother used, and her worn-to-a-thread quilts soothe better as well. Yes, nostalgia pulls on the cords of a past, fondly remembered time. Memories shine through in objects that keep

FAR LEFT: Invite friends over for tea at a table set with rich, royal hues, exotic fruit, and loads of freshly baked goodies. A table runner draped over fabric remnants pulls together the look.

LEFT: Assorted treasures can appear as if they were meant to be together when they share coloring, themes, or a period.

customs alive. This is just one reason we have difficulty tossing things that may not serve an immediate need in today's environment. While our attachment to the past can lead to a cluttered home if we aren't careful, our nostalgia and the interest with which history endows items can be used to great benefit in a modern home. Take, for example, the crocheted milk jug covers those high-mannered Victorians used to drape over their cups to prevent flies from drowning in their tea. Chances are you won't see many milk jug covers on a twenty-first-century table; however, these fine items can serve myriad new functions, from acting as coasters to accenting pieces that heighten the beauty of a perfume bottle display. Revel not only in the fact that an antique quilt offers warmth and a French enamel pitcher serves lemonade but also that they link you to a past time and place, and may spark your mind to wonder about the previous owner and to imagine his or her life. When a banal object can inspire you, its purpose exceeds beauty and comfort. You've made a deliberate choice to live with enchantment.

A Soft and Romantic Look

Keep in mind that Vintage Vavoom isn't solely steeped in the past. Floor-to-ceiling antiques give a home a museum quality, a feeling that the rooms should be cordoned off with velvet ropes. At the same time, authentic romance can't be found exclusively in new, mass-produced items. "One needs the time-worn elements to soften the sharp lines of modern pieces," says *Romantic Homes* contributor Carolyn Westbrook. "Mixing in mirrors, glass, and mercury glass is a great way to compose a fabulous blend of the old and new. An antique rug with a mirrored coffee table topped with beautiful antique silver trays, which hold mercury glass, is a great way to mix the two styles for a more modern yet romantic look."

Fine-quality linens are always go-to pieces when you want to soften a room. Add a clean, tranquil look with pillows, throws, bedding, and lacy towels, whether they are newer purchases or have been in the family for generations. "Neatly fold them in all the same size and stack in small piles, then place the piles in a neat row across the top of a cabinet or behind the glass doors of a newer, more modern piece of furniture," suggests *Romantic Homes* contributor Elizabeth Maxson.

Natural elements always have a place in a home with flair. Fresh flowers, seashells, feathers, and fruit are neutral design elements that truly enliven a display. Adding fragrance, texture, and the softest notes from the outdoors, objects from nature punch up a room, bring it to life, and hint that the owner respects the natural order of things. Combining flowers with your best china or grandest vase surely gives these star attractions notable billing.

OPPOSITE: A sunny window sets ablaze sweet garden roses in a transferware pitcher.

ABOVE: In her St. Louis store, Elizabeth House, Elizabeth Maxson features vintage books and photos to add romance and nostalgia to a setting. Pull in decorative soaps with dried flowers to enhance the look.

ABOVE: Kitschy pastries play into the whimsy when served on vintage china.

The Old with the New

Today's trends, whether a certain color scheme or a unified motif, can freshen those vintage pieces you already own. Undoubtedly, the designer of today's decorative pieces was inspired by the past; hence, the well-made modern versions inherently work with your older pieces. Even the pink-and-white swirled doughnuts bought in the bakery section of your grocery look very top-drawer when served on your best china. It's a playful mix of young and old that shows personality, like sugar cubes punched up with pastel jelly beans.

A Personalized Living Space

Draw the unexpected into your home, and you may find that it perfectly expresses your sense of humor or whimsy. Sequined Indian slippers, children's books you don't have the heart to part with, glass lamp shades, and an I-don't-know-what-it-is-but-I-must-have-it porcelain figurine found at a flea market are all great accent pieces. Transferware pitchers may recall another time, but their classic appeal never flags when showcased in a perfectly lit setting.

Elizabeth Maxson has an established look; she is known for her love of warm sepia tones that make a space appear to be glazed with melted butter. Maxson's affinity for pocket watches, antique calipers, black-and-white photographs, architectural salvage, the soft lighting of a bedside lamp, and fine soaps creates the look so beloved in her shop, Elizabeth House. Chances are that you, too, either associate yourself with a particular style already or have one inside that you can tap into for the first time while decorating your home. If you are drawn to an item, it most likely has a connection to the other things you've collected.

"Draw the unexpected into your home, and you may find that it perfectly expresses your sense of humor or whimsy."

What is most distinctive about a home with Vintage Vavoom is that no other home is like it, and it is as telling about the person who lives there as a photo album can be. Yes, visiting such a home can be voyeuristic: the crooked stacks of heavy books about rose gardens; the delicate perfume bottle collection; the black-and-white photos framed in silver crying out for a polish; Blue Willow china brightening the cupboards; a yellow princess phone on the bedside table in the master suite; a rocking chair with a missing arm and an elaborately carved back. A home invites you to know more about the dweller in all his or her humor, interests, and brilliance. This sharing of intimacy with visitors is a founding principle in a comfortable home.

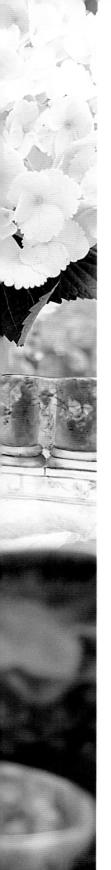

Affordable Treasures

Notice how cost isn't a requirement for Vintage Vavoom. Sure, Steuben, Meissen, and Scalamandré are buzzwords that make eyes light up, but that's too easy. Part of the fun of decorating is the story behind a piece's acquisition. "I took a walk down Fifth Avenue, saw a wonderful silver tea caddy in the Tiffany's window display, and bought it" isn't as interesting as how you made a serendipitous purchase at a garage sale.

Keep stylish decorating affordable by buying basics from big-box stores to supplement your hard-won treasures. Don't feel bullied to relegate those longtime keepsakes to the Dumpster just because they may not be of the moment. (No doubt you'll find that someone with an eye for a good piece will snatch them up!) If an item is of good quality and speaks to you, you will find a place for it. When it has lost its luster or just doesn't seem to fit in your current surroundings, store it for a time when it comes back into your design favor; reuse naturally keeps your style affordable.

Unconditional Love

If you step into a house where a pile of letters makes chaos in a room, a box of Raisin Bran throws the kitchen into disarray, or the spilled wax of a candle puts the entire dwelling on red alert—that home does not have Vintage Vavoom. Imperfections—from original hardware that may squeak to crooked doors or chipped china—add character. All the little boo-boos come with stories to share and laugh over.

In a society where walls frequently smell of fresh paint and kitchen drawers open with the purring maneuverability of a race car, Vintage Vavoom is a reminder that it is okay—even encouraged—to live with things that may appear defective to a Realtor's eye. Rather than fixating on unattainable perfection or striving to stay current to the second, choose palettes that bring you a sense of calm, and surround yourself with things that make you melt inside.

Motley china patterns are part of the Vintage Vavoom look.

Thoughtfully displayed heirloom linens are given their proper venue in a weathered armoire with punches of muted colors.

Bringing in the Vavoom
DREAM DIARY WORKSHOP

To discover your personal vavoom preferences, do the following exercises. Just sit down in a comfortable spot and get started. Set aside plenty of time to get your thoughts down on paper now, but you should also feel free to add other ideas as they come up later on. This map will be a tool to help you bring Vintage Vavoom into your home and reflect your personality in your décor.

1. Start by making a list of items that remind you of happy times—from your childhood, favorite vacations, beloved relatives' homes. Simply allow yourself to list items you loved (or love), special rooms, and any specifics that come to mind, without stopping to judge or edit yourself. Just keep writing. Make sketches if you'd like. When you feel as if you've come to the end, take a quiet moment and see if any more thoughts come up. Write those down, too. When you're done, you will have created a very thorough "favorites" list.

2. Now, take a look at your writing and see if there are any common themes. Did you gravitate toward the kitchen? The front porch? Certain collectibles? A certain period of history? Colors? Shapes? Compile a list of all the themes arising from your "favorites" map.

3. File your favorites map and lists of themes in the "Bringing in the Vavoom" section of your binder. Add more paper and ideas as they come. Remember: This is your personal workbook. Let yourself dream!

2

QUALITY COUNTS

Recognizing Well-Made and Important Pieces

No matter how many beautiful pieces have been passed down to you, you'll undoubtedly have the great opportunity to collect most of the pieces that compose your dwelling. This is one of the true pleasures in creating a romantic home.

Vintage furnishings come with rich, textured tales that are lovingly told—or possess a delicious mystery we may never uncover. Well-chosen mass-produced items also have their place in our homes, and they help balance function and affordable beauty. Do a background check before buying anything.

BE DISCERNING. ASK HOW THE PIECE IS MADE AND decide whether you want it to fulfill a trendy whim or whether it is something you want to live with forever. Read up on and research antiques you are interested in acquiring. Use some of the resources available to you—dealers, shopkeepers, books, magazines, and the Internet—to become more knowledgeable about a decorating field that interests you.

PRECEDING PAGE: An Eastlake wall shelf displays prized pieces of Sandwich glass and French bleu celeste Sèvres porcelain.

ABOVE LEFT: Mixing your favorite flowers is as pretty as any arrangement from a florist.

ABOVE RIGHT: Outdoor furniture is given an unexpected jolt when layered with treasured pillows.

OPPOSITE: Grouping your favorite themed pieces creates an inviting outdoor nook.

PEDIGREE

The first mark of distinction for a valuable piece is its maker. If it was manufactured by a luxury goods company such as Tiffany, Lalique, or Wedgwood, its value significantly increases. Provenance, the previous ownership and history of an object, is another indicator of value. *Romantic Homes* collectibles editor Nancy Ruhling says, "If the piece comes from a famous house or belonged to a noted figure or a celebrity, that fact adds greatly to its value."

CRAFTSMANSHIP

The way something is made is the best indication of how well it will stand the test of time. A mahogany chest nailed together most certainly promises a longer life than one made of pressed wood and carpenter's glue. A hand-painted jug, even with a chipped handle, has more value than a pitcher bought at a nationwide home décor chain store. And there is a reason why the linens your grandmother used for her holiday table setting still hold court on your table: because they were made with fine materials and cared for by someone who respected them.

TOP: Detailed needlepoint pillows depicting favorite animals add whimsy.

ABOVE: A vintage child's game can add energy, personality, and color to any room.

OPPOSITE: Your best china will always add beauty to a space.

educated consumer course

Ask Questions

A professional shopkeeper is your go-to person on a piece's provenance. Ask where he or she found the piece and if it has been refurbished. If the shop carries more than one style of that piece, find out how well each sells.

Inspect

See how the piece was made, and look for markings that indicate the artisan or company that produced the piece. As in life, you can learn a great deal by looking below the surface. When Carolyn Westbrook shops for high-quality pieces, she is careful to note how old they look. Was the furniture put together with staples, screws, nails, or square nails? (Square nails represent age, whereas screws and staples signify a newer item.)

Be careful not to have the piece refinished or repaired, as those treatments could diminish its worth. In many cases, when a piece has a reputable provenance, a blemish or an imperfection adds value.

Research

If you collect or want to begin collecting a specific style, read books, trade publications, and auction catalogs and visit websites to inform yourself about what to look for. Speak to reputable sellers who offer items in your collecting field of interest.

Befriend

Strike up a relationship with your favorite shopkeeper, dealer, or auction appraiser. See yourself as an apprentice, and ask him or her to guide you on what to look for in a piece and help you acquire those hard-to-find pieces you have your eye on.

Feel the Connection

If you are considering a purchase and find that you dream about it, that piece speaks to you. Whether it costs $5 or $500, you have to love it to live with it. Be wary of trends, but let your instinct guide you.

Sure, "blowout sales" and "50% off" signs make the most discriminating shopper weak in the knees, but will a good bargain be a valued addition to your home? Is it something you can see yourself passing down to future generations? If so, great, but you'll actually save money if you restrict yourself from buying the latest fads that will never be used and instead buy something of value that will always have meaning because it's exceptional. As Carolyn Westbrook says, "Today, people have become influenced by price, instead of asking themselves if they are making a good investment. I was once asked, 'What's the difference between 100 percent linen and plain cotton?' My response was, 'The same difference as paper and plastic.'"

Set on its own, vintage silverware tells a unique design story.

INVESTMENT
PIECES

When investing in rare items, begin by considering your budget. Determine how much you are able to spend, and then shop around for the best buys. Acquire pieces as your budget permits so as not to be overwhelmed by extreme expense. The very word *collection* implies that the items were gathered over time. A person who buys a ready-made collection is an affront to the true collector. The thrill is in the accumulation of pieces, by traveling to different shopping venues or winning an item on an online auction. Finding the perfect addition to a growing group will become a lifetime hobby.

"Many of us do not have the means to invest in a piece that will appreciate over time and then later becomes an investment piece. This is not a bad idea if someone has the funds. However, I caution my clients from turning their homes, their havens, into a living bank account," says Elizabeth Maxson.

ABOVE: Hydrangeas, grapes, and pears accentuate the yellow-green hues of the Vaseline glass bowls, stemware, and Sanibel dishes.

OPPOSITE: This Hoosier cabinet full of glassware adds panache to the kitchen area.

ABOVE: Spools of thread aren't just for sewing anymore. Throw a handful into a small basket to create a colorful look.

LEFT: Fill a favorite teapot with flowers and pair with vintage handkerchiefs and tea cloths for a cozy cottage vignette.

LEARNING CHANNEL

To truly learn a collectible's value requires a lesson in history. In fact, the decorative arts *are* history, part of a rich and involved story. The events are just as romantic, with sociological implications that can educate you about another time and place. Many of us treasure old things because they connect us to an illustrious past that we find inspiring. This is precisely why furnishings that haven't been restored hold such value: Our imaginative side can actually feel and use the piece exactly as intended by the original owner. While some

people may prefer to be the sole owner of a furnishing, many of us delight in the musty fragrance seeping from the wood of a French armoire or the imprecise blemishing in a mercury glass mirror.

For a beginner collector, museums, auction houses, historical homes, and flea markets offer a formidable education. By familiarizing yourself with a variety of collectibles, you can home in on your true desires. Additionally, you'll learn why two pieces that look alike at an antique store may have vastly different prices. One piece may be signed by a reputable manufacturer, or made in a rare color. The other might possess a hairline crack or an imperfection seen only after close inspection. Such thoughtful investigation becomes an exercise in what influences cost and value.

Nancy Ruhling says, "The best collections comprise the best pieces. To distinguish between good, better, and best doesn't cost anything and sharpens your eye."

TOP: A beautiful French figurine guards a footed cake plate piled high with miniature apple pies.

ABOVE: Decorating with Staffordshire dogs punches up any drab space with color, texture, and wonderful history. Sue Sparks acquired hers on a trip to Scotland, enticed by them as wonderful keepsakes of a memorable trip.

As pretty as your best silk scarf, this fabric transforms a run-of-the-mill chair into your home's most coveted accent piece.

PASSING THE TEST

The most important test of a piece's worth is your own feelings toward it. If you love it, then it has value. Keep your watchful investor's eye on the stock market, as any auction appraiser worth his or her fancy job title will tell you not to buy art as an investment. Consider the definition of *decorative item*—something that is meant to be admired, something that adds beauty to your home. Says Ruhling, "If the piece says *take me home*, by all means, do so."

If you are lucky enough to find something you love, its price becomes secondary. Says Maxson, "I often see people who want so badly to add something special to their home, but [they think] it doesn't go with their style. That is an oxymoron! Whatever they fell in love with *is* their style." She further says that an item is meant to be enjoyed rather than fussed over like a fragile showpiece. "Many wonderful antiques can be used that will definitely appreciate over time, such as silver and china," she adds.

ABOVE: Interesting produce set atop artistic dinnerware creates a striking tabletop.

OPPOSITE, ABOVE LEFT: A great coffee-table arrangement can be comprised of the most banal of objects, such as old journals and postcards.

OPPOSITE, BELOW LEFT: When it comes to creating simple beauty, sometimes less is more.

OPPOSITE, BELOW RIGHT: A cornucopia of fruits, pastries, and other delights is even more tempting when displayed on different levels and a layering of textiles.

FALLING FOR TRENDS

If you fall for the latest trend but are unsure if it will be outmoded by the time you place it

on the checkout counter, save the expense and buy a mass-produced piece that you can dis-

play and use until the trend passes. Examples are an

oversized railroad clock, made to look old, that takes up

valuable space, and colorful spotted dishware that is

perfect for one festive gathering but may cause your

eyes to blur after regular use. "Mix expensive things

with inexpensive things, but [the result] needs to look

> "Something that is expensive may not show attractively, while an inexpensive item can really shine."

good and have balance. Something that is expensive may not show attractively, while an inex-

pensive item can really shine. You have to follow your own instinct. It's what you feel, your

inner self that comes through," says Hilde Leiaghat of Pom Pom Interiors in Los Angeles.

KNOW THYSELF

Do not be swayed by outside influences. "It is important for collectors to know themselves

well enough to know if they truly love something because it is a trend, because their

friends love it, or because they just want to fill a space with the right piece," says Maxson.

Remember why you are purchasing the item, and don't shop on impulse. Maxson herself

offers one of the more extreme examples: She once lived without dining room chairs for

almost four years because she knew what she wanted and wouldn't settle for anything else.

Though not expensive, they were difficult to find.

Quality Counts
DREAM DIARY WORKSHOP:
BUILD ON YOUR FAVORITES

Become better informed about what *quality* means to you, and you'll be sable to make smarter decisions when shopping for your home.

1. Create a "sky's-the-limit" list—items you love no matter what the price. Ready—go! Maybe certain iconic words will come to mind: Tiffany, Lalique, silk, mahogany. Or you may be inspired by simpler terms: stained glass, cut crystal, gauzy cottons, unpainted pine. Think of details from recent shopping trips, friends' homes you love, and show houses you've seen, as well as items you've always wanted to purchase. List them all. Also, remember that when you love something, your passion is "quality" enough. You will continue to make additions to your list, so add blank pages to this section of your workbook. Referring to this list will help you be more discerning when you are at antiques malls and thrift stores, or even in your own attic.

2. Take a stack of magazines (that you don't mind ripping apart), and pull out pages that illustrate your quality list. You may clip an ad for the exact item, or maybe a certain pattern or layout will catch your eye. Three-hole-punch these and add them to the binder under "Quality Counts." Continue to add to this section as you find other clippings. If you like, you can also illustrate your list by cutting out the pictures and gluing them on a sheet of paper to make a collage.

3. Take stock of your knowledge and "go back to school." Do you love certain antiques or collectibles but need to know more in order to be an informed buyer? Do you know the best places to buy vintage linens, for example, if they're one of your favorites? Start keeping notes in this part of the binder, listing resources like shopkeepers and knowledgeable acquaintances. If you decide to attend some classes, keep your notes in this section for future reference, too. Write down book titles and list other relevant sources.

3

SHOPPING

Where to Go, What to Look For, and How to Shop

When a shopper steps into a store, she is in search of something, whether the perfect piece or decorating ideas. Consider your shopping outings as one giant treasure hunt. You may have a general idea of what to expect, but you may encounter twists and turns that lead you to alternate discoveries. No matter where your quest takes you, it's enlightening and enjoyable, and can lead to riches beyond your expectations.

IN TODAY'S MARKETPLACE, THE CHOICES CAN BE OVERWHELMING. We have chain stores, specialty boutiques, the Internet, flea markets, estate sales, auctions, and antiques stores. The good shopper familiarizes herself with all her available options and returns to the scenes of her greatest successes. Shops not only offer items to add to your collections, but they are also a fantastic venue to inspire you with their creative displays. Shopkeepers are great experts to learn from, and this chapter will teach you how to take full advantage of your excursions.

PRECEDING PAGE: At antiques malls, estate sales, and flea markets, buy mismatched silverware and group together for true vintage appeal.

ABOVE LEFT: When shopping, think about how to use ordinary items in extraordinary ways in your own home. This vintage box spring, for example, has infinite possibilities.

ABOVE RIGHT: Antique spools of thread that pay homage to a past era are one of those unexpected treasures you can find on a shopping hunt.

OPPOSITE: An assembly of weathered finials is so eye-catching you may not purchase them for their intended use.

You never know what treasures you will find when hunting in shopping venues such as the Monticello Antique Marketplace in Portland, Oregon. Even thimbles with whimsical motifs can create a beautiful display.

ANTIQUES MALLS

Antiques malls are a wonderful place to shop because they showcase a variety of great finds in one concentrated location. For example, at the Monticello Antique Marketplace, located just outside the city district of Portland, Oregon, dealers have done most of the scouting for you. "We have collectors, brand-new homeowners, regular customers, and destination travelers," says owner Kelli Riedman. Arbiters in design shop such venues frequently in search of one-of-a-kind objects or inspiration for next spring's production cycle, when the stores they work for will recreate the originals. By shopping at these spots, you can be the originator of a trend and actually own the bona fide find. Rather than buy a leather suitcase made to look old, why not buy the real thing? Originals abound in stores with distinctive

selections such as Monticello. Your eyes bounce from one shelf to the next, and you'll soon find yourself stacking up goodies in your wire basket as if they were food items in a grocery store.

Part of the fun is that you can go without even knowing what you are in the market for. Old croquet mallets, vintage cooking utensils, silverware, and postcards may fuel a new collecting passion or just add the right touch to a neglected corner in your home. Though prices at antiques malls may not be as competitive as those at flea markets, browsing through a diverse, well-edited selection is a significant convenience. Also take advantage of the liberal shopping environment, where dealers may be willing to negotiate on price.

how to shop an antiques market

❧ When searching for specific items, make a list. It can be overwhelming when you're confronted by the enormous inventory of an antiques mall. Educate yourself as much as possible about what you're looking for. Does the piece have any markings or identifiable characteristics? A dealer may be completely unaware of what he has, or perhaps thinks something is what it is not.

❧ If you are looking for something specific, go ahead and ask. An employee or a dealer may know where it is hiding. If he does not know, or thinks he does not have any—look anyway. He might have missed it, or you may find an unexpected treat.

❧ Don't be afraid to dig. Many dealers fill their spaces to the brim. Look through bins of fabric and shelves of books. A full space just means lots of treasures are waiting to be found.

❧ Allow yourself plenty of time to look around. Antiques malls are always filled with unexpected distractions.

❧ Get ideas from booth displays for use in your own home.

❧ Bring a friend. It is always good to get a second opinion, and your friend may see something you missed. Choose a friend with a large car to help you transport your finds home!

❧ Take pictures. Sometimes it's hard to imagine a find in your own home. A camera can help you try before you buy.

❧ If you like a place, make frequent visits. Dealers are constantly restocking their booths with new treasures. Get to know the employees, who will be more likely to recognize things you like and let you know about them.

PRECEDING PAGE: Ironware is a big seller at antiques stores and architectural salvage shops, where this farmhouse vignette can inspire a collection.

ABOVE: The charm of any collectible can be heightened by the perfect setting and lots of natural light.

LEFT: Even antique croquet mallets can be a decorative find—the ideal treasure, as they can be both used and admired.

TIME TO FLEA

Flea markets have always attracted the passionate shopper, and many people have made a profession of frequenting such venues, which are sprinkled throughout the country, even the globe. Typically held on the weekends, either in fields stitched with tents or on school playgrounds, flea markets bring together dealers and collectors in a friendly exchange of goods and services. For information on noted flea markets, see the Resources guide.

To shop a flea market successfully, keep in mind the following:

- *Arrive early, even before sunrise, and bring a flashlight.*

- *Walk through the entire market once and then home in on the dealers whose goods struck your fancy.*

- *For outdoor flea markets, dress accordingly and in layers. Wear comfortable shoes and carry rain gear for inclement weather.*

- *Prepare a list of items to narrow your search.*

- *Don't settle for the asking price. State your offer and be prepared to walk away rather than be bullied into making a purchase.*

- *Bring cash. Although some dealers accept credit cards, cash goes further and will help you in your bargaining. You can even ask for a cash discount.*

- *If you see something you are interested in but are not happy with the price, don't buy on impulse. You may get it at a reduced rate if the item hasn't been sold by the end of the day, when vendors are more inclined to negotiate in order to unload their goods.*

- *Visit markets throughout the country, as some items are more plentiful in certain regions than others.*

OPPOSITE: A great piece offered at an antiques shop has natural weathering from being displayed outdoors.

LEFT: The timeless starfish is given its proper venue when grouped in abundance in a vintage wire basket.

TOP: Vintage American-made pocket watches are inviting embellishments and can be found at estate sales.

ABOVE: A beautiful shop display can inspire your own home decorating.

OPPOSITE: An example of a shopkeeper's use of old postcards and pages from a book to yield a creative display.

GREAT SAVES

Another bonus in buying vintage is the savings. Most likely you will receive an authentic, one-of-a-kind piece at a price better than the reproduction. However, though fun, the hunt requires initiative. Unless the item is something you have had your eye on, it's not necessary to spend a lot of money. Designer and dealer Alicia Paulson, who started a collection of miniature vintage chairs because she had *the* shelf that was the perfect display venue, recommends going to Goodwill and consignment shops as well as estate sales and antique malls. If you go regularly and take your time, these places can be treasure troves.

A GOOD IDEA

A well-appointed store is a formidable source for ideas. Stores can be as visually enticing as a spread in a home décor magazine, with lush displays that are ready to inspire—a dramatic contrast to the motley arrangements in a flea market or an antiques mall! The job of a good shopkeeper is to create magic with his or her merchandise, finding inventive ways to display

CLOCKWISE FROM TOP LEFT: The man-made and the natural play a perfect symphony of light and beauty. • Finding myriad ways to decorate, such as pairing cloches with natural elements, is a hallmark of personal style. • Vintage scales have become trendy collectibles in recent years. • This 1780s lion sofa bed from Sweden, with custom finish and upholstery, sets the stage and color palette for a lush vignette. • French soap in large, uneven blocks, vintage lace, and dried flowers create an old-world feel in the bathroom.

moonlighting

Shop for pieces that do double duty:

🐚 A Victorian cruet becomes an innovative vessel for your flowers when you place stems in each glass.

🐚 Apothecary jars or glass candy dishes showcase your collection. Lace, buttons, and game pieces—even ornamental fruit and vegetables—become instant décor under glass.

🐚 Old scales or cake plates can be used as display stands to add height.

🐚 Lace remnants and textiles embellish pieces and add a vintage feel.

🐚 Glass salt and pepper shakers can hold powder and fine toiletries such as bath salts.

🐚 A beveled mirror can be used as a tray for hors d'oeuvres, or set bath salts on your vanity.

🐚 Mixing bowls are perfect vessels for chunky soaps and sea sponges.

🐚 Metal flower frogs are great for displaying family photos.

items and make the ordinary look like masterpieces. One technique shop-keepers employ is to section off spaces and compose styled vignettes—an assortment of linens in red, white, and blue; hand-colored prints from a book strewn on a silver tray; or playing cards showcased in a toast rack. Beautifully wrapped boxes are another common technique to elevate items, while stacks of dinnerware always delight the eye.

Elizabeth Maxson's store, Elizabeth House, is literally crammed with inspiring ideas. Like the sepia tones of an old photograph, a few muted colors soften the mass of things. Lace is draped here and there, vintage spools of

ABOVE LEFT: These Cavallini & Co. cards are made to look old, which suits an iron toast rack sold at Seattle's Watson Kennedy.

ABOVE RIGHT: The Monogram Shop in East Hampton, New York, may be as big as a diva's closet, but the focus on high-quality objects and thoughtfully produced vignettes express a lovely creative flair.

OPPOSITE: Finding inspiration in colors and patterns is easy at a well-appointed shop.

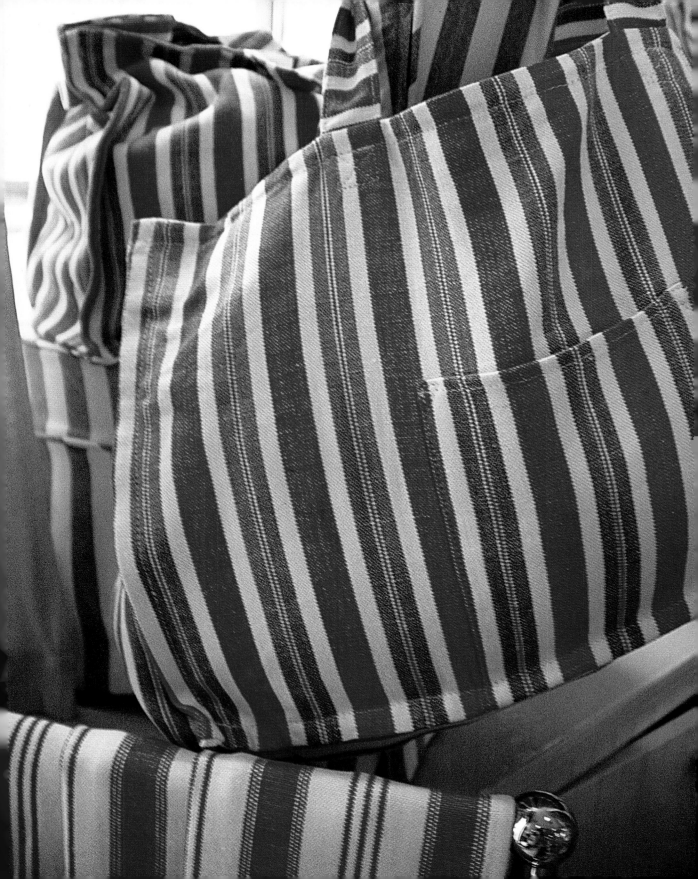

thread become high art, and dried lavender and velvet ribbons add to the old-world flavor. Maxson has an eye for using the banal in innovative ways, such as old metal flower frogs to display family photos. "Or make a statement with fresh wall art," she says. Maxson will take a single collection, such as vintage jewelry, old family photos, pocket watches, or vintage eyeglasses, and arrange the items in a shadow box. She will hang them in a uniform manner, typically from floor to ceiling, which certainly has an eye-catching effect. "But how fun with vintage items!" she says.

Not restricted to visual impact, shops play with other senses as well. Deliciously scented candles or the nostalgic tunes of a French chanteuse, or perhaps Ella Fitzgerald, pull at your romantic side. Though the prices can be expensive at smaller retailers, there are always those tempting indulgences such as scented candles and linen sachets, which are as enjoyable as a hot bath and a magazine.

RIGHT: A successful shopkeeper understands the importance of display. Here, stacks of French ashtrays are aptly showcased atop a classic gingham tablecloth.

OPPOSITE: The spirit of Chicago's P.O.S.H. is featured in its back corner, which could easily be taken for Paris.

This inviting shop display shows the myriad ways to showcase items with color and a shared motif.

Flea markets, shops, and antiques malls are brewing with ideas ready to be used in your home. For example, you may have never considered kitchen bakeware pieces from the 1950s to be decorative. But when they are grouped attractively, with their colored wooden handles and worn look from frequent use a half-century ago, you may find them irresistible. Such pieces add to the personality of your home.

Once you adapt to the layout of your favorite shop, you can focus on those areas that merchandise your interests. "Have a couple of themes in mind when you shop," suggests

modern basics:
what to shop for

- ⚜ Great fluffy towels

- ⚜ Quality stationery and note cards

- ⚜ A stack of coffee-table books

- ⚜ Quality fabrics in timeless patterns such as French ticking and florals

- ⚜ A colorful apron, even three hung in a row

- ⚜ Indulgent bath salts packaged in a glass jar

- ⚜ Scented candles

- ⚜ Galvanized pitchers in whimsical bright colors and patterns

- ⚜ Blocks of hand-milled soap

- ⚜ Kitchen appliances, such as a mixer or a coffee-maker, with a nod to retro design

- ⚜ Cocktail accessories

- ⚜ Pillows and throws

- ⚜ Cake plates

- ⚜ Dishware

ABOVE: Forget buying new. All the best books come in vintage varieties for just a few dollars.

OPPOSITE: Giant tin stars are a staple of flea markets and homes with Vintage Vavoom.

WINDOW SHOP

Some of the best browsing can be done without even entering a store. Colorful window displays can be as magical as an old book of fairy tales. A variety of rose bouquets marches before an assortment of pillows in fruity colors, for example. Bowls are turned over to create height and laid over sheets of writing paper and gift cards. Noses fog up the glass as their owners try to gain a better view of the mishmash of items to purchase, paired with elements such as playing cards, frosted cookies, and bunches of yarn sprouting from cupcake wrappers. Such bold originality may not suit your home's style, but it will be stored in the part of your brain with the whimsical and the superfluous, so don't be surprised if one of those window vignettes pops up at a future time in your home.

designer Alicia Paulson. "Anything with green roses, or paintings of dogs with ribbons. Quirky things around which to build your own unique collections." Or feed on the ideas that are presented. Perhaps you will be lucky enough to make a great purchase or at least know what to look for on a future shopping excursion.

SHOPKEEPERS AS TRENDSETTERS

Without realizing it, you may have chosen the unique pistachio and mocha color combination in your bathroom or added vintage

TOP: Unusual artifacts become wonderful vignettes, such as these balls situated in a mortar and chosen for their primitive shapes and natural texture.

BOTTOM: Learn from the displays of a wonderful antiques shop, such as this store in Bridgehampton, New York.

library books to your china display because of what you saw at one of your favorite boutiques. Shopkeepers are some of the most creative originators of popular trends. "Think about it," says Maxson. "They see customers, vendors, other store owners all day, every day." Vendors have been on planes, shipped crates of worldly goods, and lavished unique items upon a willing market. Thus, such vendors are both on the forefront of what is happening and following the responses of curious shoppers. Successful sales create trends.

Take advantage of this knowledge; as a shopper, you can have a front-row view of what is happening in home style by making frequent trips to a well-appointed shop. Color is one example that drives trends. "If that color keeps popping up on merchandise," says Maxson, "that is a trend." She further describes her search for anything slate blue and chocolate. Lightning struck during a trip to Europe years ago. "It was everywhere in Brussels, and I fell in love with it," she says. However, at home in St. Louis, she had difficulty finding the dual tones in fabrics and accessories. Now the blue and brown have crossed the pond to the East Coast and beyond.

With the rise of Target and inexpensive goods made in China, the small shopkeeper is challenged to stay ahead of the trend curve for fear that his or her special little shop may have a "For Rent" sign taped to its window. Stores offer shoppers a preview of what's happening next. Take the clearance table, for example, where marked-down items are an indication of trends coming to an end. Hence, the chain retail stores are most likely promoting lower-quality versions of those very items, producing them at lower costs.

Keep in mind that modern has a place in Vintage Vavoom. New styles, products, and trends are easy ways to freshen a look, giving your home an updated feel.

THE SHOPPER'S ADVANTAGE

Once a shopper develops an inspirational rapport or connection with a shopkeeper, that relationship will even influence the way the store owner replenishes his or her merchandise. Stores typically hold trunk shows and special shopping previews that are exclusive to their better customers. They share their vast knowledge on design, sometimes even offering interior design services.

> "Modern has a place in Vintage Vavoom. New styles, products, and trends are easy ways to freshen a look."

The term *friendly shopkeeper* applies to those who direct shoppers to goods that may not be found in their own store. Maxson frequently does this because, she says, "Everyone wins. The shopper is grateful for the tip and gets what she wants, the shop owner makes a sale and in return will direct her customers to your store."

Shopping

DREAM DIARY WORKSHOP: MAKING IT HAPPEN

Your favorites and quality lists (see pages 47 and 67) will help you make better decisions when you are out shopping for home décor. Now, take a moment to write out your dream shopping destination list and some budget ideas.

1. Where have you always wanted to go shopping? Paris? London? A Sotheby's auction? The Brimfield, Massachusetts, antiques market? A charming shop you read about in a magazine? New York for window shopping? Go ahead, list away, and don't hold back! Pull out newspaper and magazine clippings about shopping destinations and put them in the "Shopping" section of your binder. Keep adding to this section. Learning about new places will give you ideas, too. Next time you plan a vacation, use this list. After you return from your trip, you can check off one dream shopping excursion.

2. Take a look at your themes and quality lists from the previous chapters. Do the research to find out the best places for acquiring some of your favorite items. Update the list as you learn more.

3. Bearing budget in mind, honestly assess your ability to start chipping away at your dream list. Maybe you already have a certain dollar amount budgeted annually for new (or vintage, but new to you!) purchases. Or perhaps you need to plan a garage sale to make room for new items and to provide you with pocket change. Maybe it's time to set some money aside each month to save up for that dream shopping trip or that one item you just have to have. Do your best—maybe there are things you spend money on now that aren't as important as others. Take time to reflect and

prioritize. Come back to this section from time to time to see how you are doing.

4. Remember that even window shopping can provide great Vintage Vavoom inspiration—and it's free! Make notes or take photos of window displays that inspire you. Then step inside the shops and take notice of the store's unique style, any new trends, the special items and best products they carry, whether vintage or new, and so on. Absorb the pros' use of color, fabrics, and patterns, and their displays of new or vintage vignettes.

5. Keep a price and product log. This is a great way to catalog favorite stores and the items they specialize in, as well as your dream item shopping list and your shopping successes. Your categories might be: (1) Price Comparison Log: similar items at different stores—to map the best prices; (2) Price Tracking: If you're planning to invest in an item, make note of price and vendor as you're doing your research. Is it going up in value? Holding steady? (3) Shopping Successes: When you've managed a great bargain, make a diary entry about your experience. Did you talk the price down directly with the vendor? Did you arrive early at an estate sale and get an entire collection of pristine vintage kitchen tools? Remember what worked for the next time! Celebrate your successes by keeping track of them.

4

❦

COLOR

Playing with the Options

Now that you've begun to gather

some finds, it's time to show them off in your home. Like launching an evening with a celebratory cocktail hour, we've dedicated the first decorating principle to color.

We capture the beauty and liveliness color brings to a space; experience homes created with individualism and warmth; and take an intimate look at places where real people dwell. Each of the residences sings an ode to the owners' heritage and desire to decorate with a love of texture, patterns, and those soft, romantic touches that make you want to sit back and stay awhile. These are the homes that wear their heart on their sleeve. Showing off, but not in a conceited sense, they willingly share their secret of how easy it is to have fun. When you are swathed in color, you get a happy, oozy, sugary feeling in your stomach. Let's begin to play!

COLORED HOUSES

Pass by a pale blue or candy pink house and you'll have a reaction, whether it instantly appeals to you or acts as a nice-place-to-visit-but-wouldn't-want-to-live-there stimulus. Colorful landmark homes typically come with a history. Painting each seaside house a different brightly colored shade was a common device so sailors could distinguish their homes on foggy days. With their flamboyant style, Victorian "painted ladies," built during the 1880s and 1890s, were painted in a variety of colors to draw attention to their architectural detailing, such as turrets and pitched roofs. The bold hues further expressed the owners' carefree approach. Many historically accurate examples still exist today. For example, the owners of the landmark home Blue Cottage in Laguna Beach, California, searched historical records to replicate the house's original shade. A row of colorful aprons and a French deck chair in cabana stripes play off the joviality of the facade's bright attitude.

PRECEDING PAGE: Patterns and colors have a reminiscent style, yet fit well in today's décor.

LEFT: A cheerful collection of aprons hanging in a row is a whimsical, practical display of color.

OPPOSITE: One multicolored piece can add a playful jolt to an already gutsy backdrop.

GETTING A LITTLE COLOR

As bold as turquoise walls or as simple as a few red tea towels, the amount of color you want to add to your home is a matter of personal preference. While you may love the way your friend's lemon yellow kitchen looks but find the shade too extreme to live with yourself, you can easily drop in your favorite shades with such nonpermanent touches as aprons, dinnerware, tea towels, embroidered hand-kerchiefs, and the trusted elements of food and flowers. Once you've established your room's foundation, these punchy accessories not only add a bright spot but also are easily changed along with your decorating moods.

A single vintage children's pail in animated colors or a jovial pitcher featuring a gnome can provide a witty touch that radiates person-ality. In fact, one well-chosen statement piece can instantly transform even the starkest of rooms. If you find a piece that you are attracted to but fear its colors may not blend with your current collections, keep it in mind for impulse decorating.

OPPOSITE: Christmas tree ornaments break out of their seasonal mode when arranged in this whimsical pitcher, where the striped candy canes complement the gnome's lollipop.

LEFT: Find colorful accessories in any vintage piece, such as an enamel children's pail used as a flowerpot.

THE BOLD AND THE
BEAUTIFUL

Color can be used as a subtle accent—or boldly. In the latter case, you'll want to choose a palette that seamlessly integrates your rooms, such as a variety of citrus tones to harmonize the overall home. Keep in mind shades of color that complement your collections. Weave in textured pieces, such as blankets, rugs, and window treatments, and decorating becomes a playful exercise. "Combining color and fabrics is not a problem for me. I feel intuitively drawn to color," says designer Alicia Paulson. Her studio, a cornucopia of fabrics, paper, crafts, childhood collectibles, and vintage pieces, features a colorful vignette in every available spot. Even an enamel

ABOVE LEFT: A simple kitchen towel can brighten an entire room.

ABOVE RIGHT: Give your grandmother's silver due justice by displaying it with a collection of colorfully embroidered handkerchiefs.

OPPOSITE: The simplest of items perk up an already colorful corner.

TOP: Otherwise unrelated items form a playful group when they all play on bright colors and patterns.

ABOVE: The icing on these pink cupcakes is a frivolous accessory that's as sweet as it tastes.

OPPOSITE: No one can resist a plate of waffles, and when they're heart-shaped, they add to the charisma of a thoughtfully set table.

tin of yarn can make one's eyes shine with pleasure. Clearly, Alicia is having fun with her over-the-top style, and visitors have the opportunity to see her creative whimsy at work. Chinese lanterns fall from the ceiling, while her handmade crocheted slippers hang happily on the wall. The combinations of quirky pieces, displayed against bright backdrops, are so jolly they appear to be from a children's book. "I find it satisfying to have control of my little spaces. I feel better knowing the room is *nice*," she says.

Aside from her husband's designated rooms, Alicia continues the fun throughout her home—even a pantry or a kitchen table can become a tableau of color. Mixing a colorful tablecloth with pink cupcakes, retro candy, and fruit keeps you smiling. "The details are like ruffles and buttons on a dress, which make you feel it's special," says Alicia.

Red appears throughout the house, an accent color that links each room to the next. This technique is most prevalent in the bathroom, as the small space empha-

sizes all the important details. In addition to her chosen palette of bright blue and red, Alicia channeled the French seaside. She created a fun and functional space with gingham curtains, the cabana-striped lamp shade, and a red-and-white polka-dot box to store unsightly, useful things. She added a red Chinese lantern to the mix and made the curtains specifically for that room.

BIG COLOR IN SMALL SPACES

"Powder rooms," exclaims store owner Elizabeth Maxson, "are the one place to unleash your boldest ideas!" Ideal for experimentation, small spaces are easily transformable and need not connect to the rest of the home. "Think about it," says Maxson. "A very large room with a strong color would be too much. A much smaller space, with little walls, is the perfect place to be daring."

OPPOSITE: Channeling the French seaside, Alicia has chosen red as her home's accent color. Here, in the master bathroom, she combines treasured finds with everyday toiletries and red towels.

LEFT: This polka-dot box, which contained dessert dishes, is the perfect place to store out-of-place belongings.

lighten up

Here are some easy ways to bring color into your home:

- Decorate with natural elements such as colorful flowers, fruit, and plants.

- Display colored glass against a window to catch the light.

- Choose accessories, such as kitchen appliances, in bold colors to add zest to a neutral room.

- Be experimental with smaller rooms and transform them from drab to dramatic.

- Consider accessories, such as a quilt or a throw, for a pop of color.

- Play with color combinations. From paint choices and fabrics to an arrangement of flowers, unexpected mixes such as blue and orange or pale pink and red can personalize a room's look.

CLOCKWISE FROM TOP LEFT: An assemblage of fruit, candy, and colored milk-glass pieces add cheer to a country kitchen. • The foods you serve are perfect complements to your inspirational setting when chosen for color and texture. • Granny Smith apples and jadeite combine beautifullly in the kitchen, sharing natural hues and shiny textures. • Bring the outdoors in with natural foods. • Open the windows to let a new season roll into the fun. • Any piece can rise to stardom when showcased on a cake stand. • Milky pink accessories are a soft balance to the vintage mint green touches.

Romantic Homes contributor Carolyn Westbrook also advocates painting a tiny room a strong color. "Suddenly no one is noticing the tiny room," she says. "They are noticing *the* room." Westbrook painted a powder room black and added a white linen shower curtain, a huge Venetian mirror, and a chandelier; it became the most stunning room in the house. "Who cares if it is tiny?" she poses. "Color can make the difference between a mundane room or a dramatic, beautiful room, where all will want to linger."

> "Go for flowers that are especially bold to reinforce the imaginative look."

ENTERTAINING IDEAS

If you've caught the color bug, a good time to play with color is when you entertain. Start with what you already own. Enliven your basic white china with just a few sunny pieces, such as a polka-dotted cake plate and dessert dishes. Weave in bright hues with place mats and linens, and consider what you serve, too. Of course, no one will turn away a chocolate cake, but pink cupcakes add to the frivolity. Choose a theme to inspire your palette, such as a 1950s diner, and you'll start to see complementary accessories everywhere you shop. Go for flowers that are especially bold to reinforce the imaginative look.

TOP: Like works of art, hand-loomed "primitive" linens lend timeless beauty to a table setting. Add a hint of sophistication to the table by offsetting fine china with dark, dramatic pieces.

ABOVE: Cocktail napkins are colorful accessories that set the right mood.

LEFT: All it takes to make a bold statement is one fabulous piece of furniture, punched up here with a bouquet of flowers in deep hues.

ABOVE: Unlikely color combinations are linked with a pink accent that connects to the velvet couch.

COLOR COMBOS

As trendy as designer handbags, some color combinations are outmoded as quickly as fashion's capricious impulses. While it's fun to fall for trends, stick primarily to your favorite palettes and try combining them with unpredictable shades. You can find inspiration in things you already own, what's being shown at your favorite stores, and nature. Practice color combinations with flowers. For example, pairing a couch upholstered in fuchsia velvet with a floral arrangement containing one flower in a matching shade provides an unlikely yet arousing blend of purple and yellow. Always choose a highlight color found in your main pieces, and then drop in other colors that add depth.

Vintage paintings and a variety of textures and patterns make a striking impression in this sitting room.

To find a combination that works for you, study what's happening in today's designs. Don't limit yourself to what you see in homes; observe the storefront awnings of your favorite boutique, stationery, and clothing stores, and check out current fabrics. Every designer works from what he or she is currently seeing; knowing this can assist you in finding an interesting blend that is distinctly modern. (See Chapter 3, "Shopping," for more details.)

SOOTHING PALETTES

Colors can be loud and extroverted or soft and soothing. Pastels always evoke a calm, serene feeling that is enhanced by the right accessories and soft lighting. Gauzy lamp shades, chandeliers with dimmers, and chiffon curtains add an ethereal tone to your palette. This spearmint-painted bedroom sets the right tone for all things rosy. A hand-colored photograph on a bedside table is very Vintage Vavoom, especially with its pistachio backdrop, which picks up the jade glass butter dish used for flower clippings. "Bright, colorful photographs of family are personal and add color," says Elizabeth Maxson.

RIGHT: Soft notes such as pastel pinks and greens, mainstays of a delicate rose, make this a romantic bedroom.

OPPOSITE: A family photo chosen for its pistachio-colored background fits perfectly in this bedside vignette. Simple flowers from the garden add soothing color and fragrance.

SEASONAL COLORS

Just as our food palette and wardrobe change with the seasons, so does our use of color. While it's unlikely that you'll redecorate your entire home for the season, pull in natural additions and buy linens and accessories that fit your seasonal impulses. It's amazing that many things you own can seamlessly integrate into a lovely vignette if you remain true to a basic color theme. While orange and brown may not be your favorite colors, adding them in the form of ribbons, leaves, and nuts will get you into the spirit of the season. Or you may want to revel in a seasonal color year-round.

OPPOSITE: Use a delightful dish towel to brighten a table set with apricots and rich Belgian chocolates.

TOP: A classic Spode china pattern brings seasonal color to your table vignette.

CENTER: A pile of antique linens and pillows makes an inviting vignette atop a vintage suitcase.

BOTTOM: Etched crystal is illuminated with nutty offerings. The silver lids are given seasonal color with the right ribbon.

Colorful beaded garlands look lovely draped over a picture frame and as tassels on pillows or furniture.

Color
DREAM DIARY WORKSHOP: WHAT COLORS ARE YOU?

1. Take a quick stroll through the rooms in your home, focusing only on color. Make note of those beloved colors that make you feel happy or serene when you see them. Remember to open your clothes closet, drawers, and jewelry box to find your winning colors and color combinations.

2. Now, gather together the colors that match these favorites from your supply of paint chips, fabric swatches, magazine clippings, colored pens, and crayons. Set out all these items in front of you and start matching up combinations that sing to you. Maybe you will see that lime green and chocolate brown have become a new love of yours, for example.

3. Do any of these combinations jump out at you as perfect for one of your rooms? Go back and review your rooms lists. Add any color ideas or swatches to the room section as appropriate. You will start building on ideas of how to transition in your favorite colors. Perhaps you don't want to repaint your entire bedroom, but you can start with one wall—the one with the headboard of your bed against it, for example. Or you might find that a few throw pillows in the color you've chosen will do the trick perfectly on your bed. Either way, each step takes you closer to refining your style and themes to create the home of your dreams.

4. Make a collage or keep color samples you've gathered in a clear plastic sheet protector in the "Color" section of your workbook. Use one sheet pocket for each color, group of colors, and combination of colors. In this section you can also keep notes of resources like paint suppliers, faux painters, and so on. Keep adding and revising as you go along, and you will always have a great reference tool when you feel the urge to update your look using color.

5

MIX AND MATCH

The Skill of Combining Contrasting Elements

Mixing and matching brings to mind childhood pastimes— playing hide-and-seek, rearranging a dollhouse—as well as those whimsical Garanimals tags that taught children how to dress themselves without appearing like a circus clown. One of the most creative ways to decorate is by pairing unusual items that seamlessly integrate into a beautiful display. Like a quilt created from blocks of different fabrics, the elements form one exquisite, united whole.

SOME PEOPLE PREFER THE "MATCHY-MATCHY" LOOK, THE home with wallpaper coordinated to the furniture's upholstery, which further picks up the border of an area rug. Others prefer to group a variety of like-minded things, somehow achieving a pulled-together look. Whatever your preference, experimenting may result in your coziest and most inviting room.

PRECEDING PAGE AND ABOVE: Choosing pieces with primary colors and themes helps you mix and match. Contrasting patterns seamlessly integrate when they share color and texture.

RIGHT: The blue-and-white Chinese pattern on an umbrella stand is the ideal complement to the color palette of a soft bedroom.

HOW TO DO IT

When decorating a bedroom, can you match a rug with the bold stripes of a rugby shirt to a classic toile bedspread? Though at first glance their partnership may appear as unlikely a match as a fox and a hound, consider the traits that unite the two textiles. The neutral colors and shared shade of midnight blue work wonderfully together. Add like-minded pieces, with the same coloring and textures, along with neutral-colored items in white and beige, to heighten the impact of your display. Continue the theme by adding other accessories, such as a blue-and-white chinoiserie umbrella holder, a mosquito net, and flowers. Romantic touches such as perfume bottles, candles, jars of bath salts, sea glass, flowers, and a crystal chandelier always make a space more inviting while also tickling the senses.

"Always keep your home refreshed and ever-changing. The right mix is a key to getting a personalized look," says Carolyn Westbrook. Depth in a room is achieved by mixing fabric textures, colors, and layers. Your rugs, drapes, pictures, and pillows are the elements to mix and match with, and they'll become the defin-

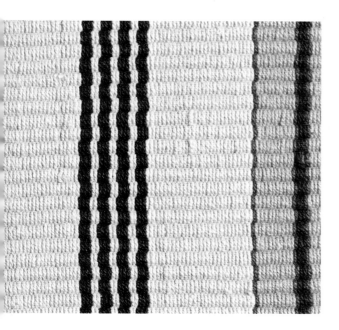

ing features of the room. Be inspired by what's happening in home décor today, such as mirrored pieces, Parisian flea market style, and vintage textiles. Consider setting a contemporary painting beside an antique mirror in an otherwise classically appointed room to create a modern focal point. Too much of any one thing is uninspiring. "The eclectic mix of masculine and feminine, primitive mixed with the elegant, and contemporary touches woven into a more traditional space only add to the beautiful unexpectedness of decorating," Westbrook says.

OPPOSITE, LEFT: An all-white palette allows you to weave in the colors and pieces of your design aesthetic.

ABOVE: Not only an exercise in color and pattern, mixing and matching can also be done through a variety of textures, as in this layered bed crowned with a sheer, romantic mosquito net.

Wicker, ticking fabric, and seashells mark the marine motif in this reading area.

White-painted vertical boards and a tone-on-tone palette of white and soft blue is punctuated with a green wood floor and a red hat that adds whimsy.

Pair trends with classics. For example, mix the old-world elegance of floral and paisley with bolder patterns such as gingham and oversized polka dots. You can even match disparate colors by linking them through an accessory. A chair slipcovered in French blue ticking looks right at home on a green-painted floor when the two are linked with the green of an ivy plant. Touches of red from the flowers in a picture and the blue-and-white transferware bowl are so subtle you hardly notice the addition of an opposing color. Unify through color, shape, pattern and motif, or style, such as vintage, romantic cottage, nautical, or Americana. A rose-printed teacup from the early 1900s, for instance, would be in perfect company with a modern version.

Once your room is complete and conveys a soothing appeal, be gutsy and consider throwing in a statement accent. It can be as grand as a door wallpapered in a patchwork collage or as simple as a red baseball hat. This is the art of mixing and matching, which gives a room charisma.

TOP: Fragrant flowers in a pewter vase and strawberries in an elegant pottery bowl add a fresh touch to this piece of historical furniture with its original paint.

ABOVE: The combination of deep royal blue and white creates a serene retreat in this master bedroom. Framed reproduction folk art and Swedish reproduction fabric add charm and appeal.

OPPOSITE: Odds and ends neatly tucked away in see-through jars bring color and whimsy to the working shelves.

While the intricate patterns on a textile may initially appear too busy to pair with anything else, focus on its color and details, and you'll find a way to match it with foreign items. A black-and-white floral canopy complements a framed picture of pages from an old book, highlighted when displayed over a deep-colored wall. Through shared color and pattern, the stencils on an antique bureau can also be lovingly grouped with textiles used as wall hangings. Chests, hatboxes, old toys—all can work so well in a display that their juxtaposition may almost seem deliberate.

Says Elizabeth Maxson, "Brightly colored marbles, beans, candy, dried peas, corn, crayons, Matchbox cars—all of these items look wonderful housed in vintage apothecary jars or even simple pickling containers. Line them up on a shelf

OPPOSITE: Spools of threads, like buttons, are an ideal way to weave color into your displays.

ABOVE LEFT: What could be more whimsical than a clear vintage jar filled with tiny buttons?

ABOVE RIGHT: An array of buttons shows that the art of mixing and matching can be accomplished inside a glass jar.

for interest and color." Finding interest in the banal is a fantastic tool for mixing and matching. You'd be surprised by the possibilities such everyday things can bestow on a vignette. That spool of thread and garments of lace may become the centerpiece on a coffee table. Stylishly packaged food items are also fantastic decorative items to freshen a look.

ALL IN THE PACKAGING

You can create one of the easiest, most inexpensive displays possible with the items you bought at the grocery store. Pair a vintage milk bottle with a plate of classic Oreos or the all-American kitsch of a Campbell's tomato soup can and French's fried onions; set them beaming cheerfully behind the glass of a vintage coffee case. If Warhol helped create Pop Art with the banal, why can't you enliven your space, too?

OPPOSITE: Even your grocery store can be a place to find decorative treasures, such as milk packaged the old-fashioned way and a plate of classic Oreos.

TOP: This polka-dotted hen happily perches beside an assemblage of flags.

ABOVE: No need to hide basic items in your kitchen's pantry when the kitsch and color add to a kitchen display.

An old coffee tin adds retro charm.

Investigate your cupboards, where tea canisters, honey jars, and spices can be as attractive as any decorative showpiece. Consider their colors and patterns; those canned goods of corn and pumpkin may add the needed jolt to an all-white kitchen.

IN THE DETAILS

Have fun accessorizing. Composing a room depends on the same technique as adding oomph to a black dress with a vivid scarf. That perfect piece distinguishes your own style. Hilde Leiaghat of Pom Pom Interiors in Los Angeles is known for creating a look with star accessories. "You have your main pieces, but it's that final touch, the small thing, that will make everything look different," she says.

Hilde finds distinctive items in an abundance of places—from nature to Belgian antique stores—among them Christmas tree balls that can be used year-round. In fact, she eschews decorating for the holidays with novelty items specifically created for a one-time-a-year use. Consider the whimsical beauty of vintage Fourth of July decorations, Christmas lights, and painted Easter eggs, and how they blend into a home's décor whether or not the season calls for them.

There is a romantic quality in Hilde's application of soft, creamy colors and motley pieces. "You can achieve this look in many ways," she says. "With a pretty lamp and candles, for example. Textures in interiors also add depth to your home; something flat suddenly becomes three-dimensional—the rough with the soft—adding the sparkle of the right kind of lighting. By accessorizing, you turn a house into a home."

Always complete the room's foundation and then add the special touches that distinguish the home from a hotel. This is a perfect opportunity to weave in all the items you've collected and have difficulty parting with, such as jewelry boxes, vases, and candlestick holders. Even dresses or

ABOVE LEFT: Designer Alicia Paulson injects color and patterns with mannequins, a staple of her design aesthetic.

ABOVE RIGHT: A patterned door, a floral printed sweater, an umbrella, and a pillow, along with a painting, an old farm chair, a hat, and sneakers, form a living example of how unlike patterns can come together.

lingerie too pretty to stow away can be hung against a wardrobe or on a seamstress' mannequin to add another point of interest. Remember those pretty red pumps you wore once and then decided just didn't fit your style? They may be the ideal accessory to brighten up a lackluster corner. Here's your chance to get back to the childhood game of memory by pulling out the boxes of décor items you've stowed away because they were too special to part with. One of them may offer the ideal touch to a complete a look.

BOOK DEAL

Books of all kinds provide another great opportunity to mix and match. To avoid the messy stacked look that should be saved for a history professor's library, choose your books carefully and examine the space, whether it's a shelf, bookcase, coffee table, or mantel. Select books of complementary size, color, and scale, then organize them in a clean grouping. When you particularly want a scheme that's young and spirited, add the colorful, timeless books and games from your childhood to bring whimsy to a vignette.

OPPOSITE: The handsome design of these children's books enhances a Colonial-inspired hatbox.

ABOVE: Velvet ribbons complement the bow on the toy bear, while the rich jewel tones of the surrounding accessories express "attic chic."

"Don't restrict yourself to using traditional bookends. So many objects can double for them!"

A bookcase is a forum for color and height, where books accented by decorative elements show personal style.

Don't restrict yourself to using traditional bookends. So many objects can double for them! Crystal boxes, pottery, small vases, perfume bottles, and candles are some of the choices that can complement the bindings. Try this snappy trick: Remove the jackets and coordinate the books themselves by color and theme. And your back issues of magazines, neatly stacked by size and style, are ideal for adding depth and texture to a basic space. Decorating is a process, and tweaking and reassembling come with the territory.

NATURALLY SPEAKING

Natural elements easily enliven a room. Flowers, shells, and fruit are the final touches that give a room presence. A bouquet commands a room like a diva on the stage with her flamboyance and style. Don't feel you have to enlist your florist for a perfect arrangement. Flip through books and magazines, make a trip to your favorite floral designer for inspiration, and then create your own bouquet with a garden variety of flowers. Even your grocery store can offer a wonderful selection of out-of-season flowers.

Fruit, vegetables, and a glass filled with herbs are easy ways to bring in natural accents. Your grocery items shouldn't be overlooked, as they may hold that color or texture that ties it all together. A glass of juice will catch light as well as any mirror, and the golden color of honey, shining through a vintage jam jar, crowns a sunny window ledge. In fact, ledges are ideal places to mix and match. Consider the rule—like-minded colors, themes, and textures—and you've added a view leading to another view.

ABOVE LEFT: The colors of fruit, fresh-from-the-oven pastries, and vintage kitchen items add beauty to a feast in the works.
ABOVE CENTER: The golden hue of honey catches light perfectly, becoming a little firefly of interest on this kitchen windowsill.
ABOVE RIGHT: We find that weaving in your prized pieces not only looks attractive but also makes food taste better.

Try mixing your collections with other pieces, though keep in mind a shared color, era, or scale, as unlikely matches are united by a shared element. Classics, vintage or modern, always fit together. Consider pieces of silver like a filler flower, which can link such standout collectibles as Vaseline glass and Meissen china. Linens embroidered with similar colors also add variation. Have fun with interesting color combinations such as pink and brown, burgundy and sea mist green, weaving in fruit, flowers, even Christmas tree ornaments for whimsy and interest. Or consider vintage board games and picture books your grandmother used, which are great decorative pieces; their colors, nostalgic promise, and fine quality add beauty.

BE CAREFUL NOT TO OVERDO IT

Once you get the hang of mixing and matching, the real skill lies in the way you edit your things. Take floral patterns, for instance. While no one can deny the classic beauty of a rose-printed fabric, in excess, it can make a space look like an overrun garden. Begin with your palette and then bring in pieces here and there. Live with it for a while before you make your selections.

TOP: It's not necessary to take a time-out on style when baking. A pink pastry box, nut-brown eggs, and the bowl you ate your first bites of cereal from deliciously mix colors and textures.

ABOVE: Color and whimsy tie together the delightful items in this inviting kitchen nook.

Consider your home's overall theme and work it into all your rooms. Designer Alicia Paulson's home is eclectic and brimming with a variety of objects, but, as she says, "A friend once suggested that the color red ran through almost every room of my house like a bit of punctuation, quietly directing the activity and preventing chaos. In order to keep mixing and matching from looking like the dog's breakfast, I like to keep that color theme subtly happening." She suggests using your foundation color "to connect, direct, and emphasize what's happening collectively."

A SENSE OF PLACE

The dining room table is the ideal canvas for mixing and matching. Begin with your perfect set of china and then add other pieces to bring an eye-catching informality to the table. A bread plate bought at a consignment shop makes Wedgwood blue the accent color for your table setting, while its floral cutout motif blends nicely with the eyelet patterns.

ABOVE LEFT: Group favorite fresh flowers in like colors and place them throughout your home for panache.
ABOVE RIGHT: Designer Alicia Paulson finds an opportunity to combine colors and elements in every vacant corner of her studio. Even shadow boxes reflect her talent for combining patterns and workaday elements such as vintage sewing accessories.

If you set the table for a meal with your simple everyday dishes, serve coffee in vintage cups after dinner, suggests Maxson. This shows personal style and adds whimsy. "Each guest has a different cup as a surprise," she says.

If you are drawn to a particular color combination but find it too gutsy to implement as a permanent fixture in your home, express your creative whim through a table setting. You don't even have to make investment purchases; instead, use linens you already own, then drape them with fabric remnants for added color and texture. Tea towels can masquerade as dinner napkins, while vintage ice cream glasses serve a variety of purposes and add another dimension. Flowers heighten the look, and you can even choose foods to serve based on their color and texture. The deep burgundy of a beet salad under a curved glass of merlot, fruit centerpieces, and attractive desserts, so colorful and fun, are rich in mix-and-match possibilities. To add extra drama to your vignette, showcase a luscious recipe on a cake stand. In fact, why not use two? In a pinch, you can create your own stand by placing plates on top of overturned bowls. Once you are fully absorbed by the beauty and possibilities a diverse table offers, test other unconventional items such as a beautifully wrapped gift, cards, and garlands of beads.

TOP: A smattering of different patterns is united by color and style.

ABOVE: New plates made to look vintage are topped with a flea-market find, an exercise in perfectly pairing and creating countless tabletop possibilities.

MAKING THE OLD NEW

Manipulate pieces to your taste. If you find a chest that you love for its style but its dark wood doesn't fit with your home's scheme, paint it in a new shade, or add stencils. Look at interesting finds in new ways. For instance, a vintage doctor's cabinet can be used in a dining room to showcase your dinnerware. "Stack new, perfectly lined plates, saucers, and cups in a row and then fold new linen napkins on another shelf," suggests Maxson.

It all comes back to trusting your instincts. When you put together things you love, they always seem to relate to one another.

CLOCKWISE FROM TOP LEFT: The combination of red, white, and pale blue, as well as old-fashioned candy dishes brimming with sweets, creates the perfect table for end-of-the-summer entertaining. • Wrapped in Swedish paper with watercolor florals and tied off with wire-edged ribbon, this box is pretty enough to be the centerpiece of a tea table covered with a lace-trimmed embroidered cloth. • Creamy white paint and pretty details transformed this nightstand in one afternoon. • Brown ribbon roses accentuate a bouquet of Sahara roses, mini calla lilies, and coffee berries. • Favored childhood pieces can add vavoom to your modern table. • These edible treats take their cue from the plate they are served on.

mix and match
DREAM DIARY WORKSHOP: BE BOLD!

Educate your eye to mix and match in your own home. Learn to trust your instincts and choose items you love. Here are a few exercises to try in your workbook. It's best to do the first two exercises one after the other. You'll need to set aside about twenty minutes. You can come back to do the last part of the exercise later if you like.

1. The first exercise will help you learn to trust your instincts. Start with a stack of magazines (that you don't mind cutting up) and a kitchen timer. Set the timer for ten minutes and begin flipping through the pages, quickly ripping out any that catch your eye. Do not spend any time wondering why; later on, you'll get to analyze it. For now, no matter what the reason—color, shape, composition, even something that moves you in the overall look of a photograph—just trust your gut. Keep flipping pages and, when something on a page sings to you, rip it out and move right on to the next. At the end of ten minutes, you should have a small pile of pages to use in the next exercises.

2. Now you get to analyze your selections. Set the timer for another ten minutes. Take one page at a time from your stack and, as quickly as you can, get an impression of it. Ask yourself what moves you about it: Is it the colors? the style of the furnishings? the light in the room? several things? Group the photos into smaller piles based on the recurring qualities you begin to find. Try to do this in the ten minutes allotted, but if you need more time, keep going until you're done.

3. Have you discovered any new qualities or themes to add to your favorites and themes lists? If so, take a moment and add them to the "Bringing in the Vavoom" section of your workbook.

Next, take the piles and a pair of scissors and, whenever appropriate, cut out the item(s) you love from the page (keep full pages if it's the overall feel you like). When you've got all of the photos edited, start mixing and matching; move the pieces around like a puzzle until you get some that complement one another. Don't be critical of yourself. Simply try combinations you may not expect to work and see if they do. This is your time to play! Mix patterns and styles if color or texture unifies them, for example.

Soon you will have the beginnings of a few collages that you can build on and embellish later with fabric swatches, color chips, other textured items, or magazine clippings. These collages will be great inspiration for you as you continue discerning your personal Vintage Vavoom style. If you choose not to make them into collages, simply drop each grouping in a separate top-loading clear plastic sheet protector and put them in the "Mix and Match" section of your binder so that you have them handy for future reference. You can repeat these exercises to help you grow comfortable with following your instincts and mixing and matching.

6

DISPLAYS OF AFFECTION

Ways to Optimally Feature Your Style

It's a shame to tuck away your prettiest things, parading them only on the rare occasion that calls for them. That kind of hoarding parallels a fairy tale: the beautiful princess locked away, virtually forgotten, but when she is released for all to see—

showtime! Liberate possessions you love, too, so that you and others can lavish them with admiration and enjoy them.

Aside from investment pieces, Elizabeth Maxson lives to use things for their intended purpose. "My reasoning is that should something chip or break, it was done while having a great time. It is only a dish, after all," she says.

TAKING INVENTORY

Begin by evaluating what you already own. Even the most mundane items can make for stylish ornaments. The kitchen is a virtual treasure trove for decorative items. Iron away month-old creases in your aprons and drape them in a spot that can use a zesty punch. The fabrics, patterns, and colors will add a point of interest to the starkest space. Sprinkle in tea towels, linens, place mats, and other kitchen textiles in gorgeous patterns, colors, and textures. Vintage pieces such as coffee grinders and recipe boxes possess one-of-a-kind charm.

Look at old rolling pins and mixing spoons in new ways. Each adds an unexpected twist as part of a floral arrangement; while on their own, placed in a sturdy vessel, they look unexpectedly clean and modern.

Those who live in a space-challenged home can create focal points with shoes, bags, even pajamas. Consider hanging them from a changing screen or window. By showcasing them the same way you would a prized collection, you blend personalized style with function.

OPPOSITE, LEFT: Add cheer to any kitchen's décor with a brightly colored dish towel.

OPPOSITE, RIGHT: A vintage enamel stockpot doubles as a vase for a lovely flower and kitchen tool arrangement, perfect for a potluck lunch celebration.

LEFT: Fabrics with pretty patterns should not be banished to a remnant drawer if they add interest to a blank space.

BELOW: An antique kitchen accessory provides beauty and function.

Maxson advises you to scour your attic, drawers, and basement for the perfect pieces. "Even the special chair that doesn't go with the house—display it and use it," she says. "Nothing is more personal than a family heirloom."

A THEME ISSUE

Just as an eye-catching store window can stop you midstride, a great display in your home can make you pause. Barbara Cheatley draws on her experience as a shopkeeper when creating vignettes in her home. For the kitchen of her guest cottage, she dreamed up an Americana theme. The punchy red-and-white dishware featuring a vintage farm kids pattern blends

with the red and white polka dots on other pieces in the space. She added such elements as an American flag fan and other starred accessories to the mix, while old Coca-Cola glasses, containers of Heinz tomato ketchup, and canisters of retro candy play into the 1950s feel. Even empty jam jars are beautiful when gathered and displayed as a group. Cheatley's cabinets are easily accessible with the step stool situated nearby, providing style and function.

CHINA PATTERNS

Cupboards, hutches, glass cabinets, and open shelving are timeless ways to show your best pieces. Stacks of dishes, punched up with colorful mugs, creamers, pitchers, and collectibles, are the essence of functional décor. Again, compose your arrangements with an awareness of height, color, and pattern. Elevating favored pieces is great for showcasing them while filling blank space. Cookbooks, cake plates, and jars can be used to elevate objects, while hooks offer the perfect spot for hanging cups.

TOP: Too pretty to stow away, colorful pajamas add a playful jolt when hung in a window.

ABOVE: While a cluster of different pieces and products could, at first, appear dizzying to the eye, color, theme, and function bring the display together.

OPPOSITE: The whimsical pattern of farm kids on these plates adds cheer to any setting.

GROUPINGS

When displaying your favorite pieces, be discerning. A group of items can dazzle the eye, but one specially appointed piece featured on its own can truly bewitch. Decluttering may seem an impossibility when each item is beautiful and has its own special story, but, as we've suggested, it's important to rotate your favorite pieces to keep the look clean and inviting. If you are over Blue Willow and want to make room for milk glass, hold a garage sale, contact a dealer, sell it on eBay, or make a special friend's day by giving her an unexpected gift.

Displays can be deliberately thought out or come together by chance. When you entertain, you become familiar with neglected objects that can be used regularly. An old cookie tin and toothpicks capped with paper flags happily complement each other with their red and white stripes. Pull in a box of tea and a pitcher in your color and pattern schemes and you have a delicious vignette.

It's common to fuss over your arrangements. During photo shoots for *Romantic Homes* magazine, we are always playing with our groupings and considering height, coloring, and the way the items are leveled. A purist in some ways, Elizabeth Maxson doesn't even allow her employees to assist her when she creates her store's displays, as she can be easily distracted by their input.

ABOVE: The most basic elements add beauty when paired with like items.

OPPOSITE: Red, white, and blue is hardly a cliché when grouped with vintage accessories.

Creating a display is a meditative process. It can be a thoughtful, fastidious exercise of shifting one piece just slightly, then removing and replacing it with outside elements; a great display is rarely achieved on the first attempt. While Maxson feels her vision can be compromised by outside assistance, you may find that pointers from a friend help you achieve the look you desire.

WHIMSICAL PAIRINGS FOR A MODERN LOOK

Vintage Vavoom homes are warm, inviting, and timeless. They are filled with lush, personalized elements that work together. Why not spice them up with a hit of irony and playfulness? Mismatched wedding china fits perfectly with tiaras in a variety of heights—the perfect way to tap into our modern-day princess. "The key to bringing in vintage items is to have many similar items that are displayed in a modern way,"

These stacks of classic patterns featured at the French General store display the art of combining color and texture.

showcase those bunny figurines you can't part with. Maxson is particularly fond of vintage birdcages, which she uses to house sleek candles. "They look wonderful burning and are out of reach of small fingers." Other style tricks are to use old toile curtains as drapes on the porch; use metal flower frogs to hold family photos; and paint an old piece a strong color, such as glossy black. "Toss some bright pillows on it and pair it with a new fun ottoman to complete the look," Maxson says.

WARDROBE
CHECK

Armoires were the go-to piece in the late Victorian era, as they followed you wherever you lived. In the present day they are always scene-stealers, but rather than keep them closed, showcase the treasures inside by opening the doors. Catch visitors' eyes with a colorful stack of linens and textiles (you don't even have to hide the detergents used to care for your finer pieces!). This cornflower blue wardrobe, located in the main room of French General, a store in Hollywood, California, evokes a timeless look filled with classically

says *Romantic Homes* contributor Maxson. She further advises to arrange in straight lines and always stack neatly. The pie birds your great-aunty used to make the holiday pie are vavoom with a sense of humor, too.

"Use an old item in a new way," encourages Maxson. Transformations abound: a cast-iron garden urn, painted white, seems right at home indoors as a vase filled with fresh-picked flowers. A curio becomes the perfect venue to

patterned textiles and complementary accessories. Though few of the stored pieces are exact duplicates, they go perfectly together with their shared color and striped theme. Mix in neutral elements, such as natural-toned hemp fabrics and a basket filled with balls of twine, and you've layered the look. The backboard, papered in toile, adds another dash of style. Tucked into the storage space on top of the armoire, the red-and-white quilts, again in converse patterns, mesh beautifully.

A LITTLE BACKGROUND

Paint the backdrop of your display cabinet in a vivid color, line it with wallpaper, or add trays, larger serving pieces, and pictures to cover a bland background. Drape lace and fabric here and there for texture and depth. Distinctive collections of color, such as jade milk glass, can be paired with earthier greens when displayed over a neutral white background.

OPPOSITE ABOVE: The color of these jadeite glass collectibles offers a soothing palette in a romantic kitchen.

OPPOSITE, BELOW: Whimsy and color are right at home in this tasteful display.

ABOVE: This collection of blue-and-white china is even more charming when displayed against a bright green background.

CONSIDER PALETTES

When arranging your china, weave in the other décor schemes of the room. This blue-and-white collection stands out against the shamrock green backdrop. Though the rose-bud wallpaper and toile patterns in the room may seem contradictory, the shared color scheme saves the day. A floor, painted in the primary green shade, along with a loomed rug and pillow, finishes this one-of-a-kind vignette.

The elegant pattern of Royal Doulton Blue Willow china really stands out when displayed in the right setting. When longtime collector Rita Razo chose a yellow palette for her dining room, she found it warm and friendly. A traditional oak dining set and Rita's favorite piece, an antique dry sink, aptly showcase her vintage china, which she began collecting in the early years of her marriage. "I loved the pattern," she says, "so when I saw it in a Sears catalog, I ordered my first set—a service for eight, including a covered casserole and sugar and creamer, for forty dollars."

OPPOSITE: An unlikely color scheme shows personality in classic pieces.

TOP: An antique dry sink is the perfect place to display exquisite vintage gold-trimmed Blue Willow china by Royal Doulton.

ABOVE: Four Blue Willow platters look striking against a creamy yellow wall. A trio of pitchers sits atop an antique Danish oak serving table.

SYMMETRY LESSON

A bright statement color is only one way to highlight your pieces. A clean, modern white palette is also inviting for its sophisticated yet soothing effect. When displaying an all-white collection, add a few touches of color, such as silverware sprouting from a creamer or a statement collectible like Limoges asparagus, or you're always safe with one of our much-touted natural decorative elements like pears and flowers. From the multiple cubbies in a shelving unit featured in the store Good Goods, a dramatic shared palette unifies myriad ironware pieces, including birds, brackets, and knobs. Extremely popular today, mono-chromatic palettes—especially in neutral colors like white, black, and cream—introduce modern vavoom to your displays.

Rita took full advantage of the dining room's bay window by installing more energy-efficient glass and lace curtains to bring in soft, diffused light. A hinged door on the window seat covers a storage area where Rita hides stuff she wants to "get out of sight for awhile." She also uses the seat in the winter as a place to stand her feather trees. Vintage pillows warm the window seat and add unmistakeable personality, a much more original alternative than a cushion.

ABOVE: Needlepoint pillows bring earth tones to a brightly painted window seat.

OPPOSITE, CLOCKWISE FROM TOP LEFT: Tableware in white and glass is anything but ordinary when grouped in different levels. • Vintage cabinets brimming with white ironstone lend cottage appeal to any room. • New and vintage ironware comes in a variety of designs, including birds, brackets, and knobs. Use these pieces to create cottage vignettes throughout your home. • A punch of needed color can be found in your produce aisle. These pears, chosen for their miniature size, are the perfect natural element to bring in other colors found in this kitchen. • Intricate pulled thread and embroidered lace place mats atop an antique lace cloth perfectly complement the antique green transferware.

SHOWPIECES

As Vintage Vavoom style illustrates, any treasured object, when displayed with panache and care, can become a showpiece. Even the simplest item, properly juxtaposed in a thoughtful setting, can occupy center stage. Investment items are no different. The high-end dining room chairs in Albert Nichols's home are so functional and stylish they can be displayed on the roof deck to extend a gathering outdoors. Everything from the good silver to handsomely packaged bath products, investment pieces, and luxury goods originally intended only for special engagements can beautifully contribute impact to the everyday style of your home.

ABOVE RIGHT: This romantic rooftop garden has gorgeous views of the San Francisco Bay and cityscape, which is an elegant complement to dining room chairs used outdoors.

SHADES OF LIGHT

ABOVE LEFT: With its open and airy feel, this multipurpose room is the perfect setting for most social functions.

ABOVE RIGHT: The table setting is intentionally simple, seamlessly integrating with the other elements, such as flowers the shade of artichokes and lavender-scented sachet card holders customized with each guest's name.

The right light can make all the difference in your display. Ideally, situate your displays near a window to receive the best natural light. If your cupboard or armoire only fits in a dark space, add a decorative lamp. From bright and friendly light to a soft and romantic glow, you can easily achieve the effect you want by tinkering with the placement of the light or perhaps by adding candles and other lamps. Change their shades if you want to update a look or go seasonal. Christmas tree lights, draped along a windowsill, reliably create a soft, festive shine. Also consider adding dimmers, which allow you to play with light levels to achieve the desired mood.

Displays of Affection
DREAM DIARY WORKSHOP:
GET UP AND MOVE IT!

Experiment with displaying and rearranging your treasures in your own home. Identify goals and ideas to try in the future, too.

1. Just as the experts recommend that if you want to reorganize your home you should start with one closet at a time, here we suggest picking one section of one room for this exercise, such as a small bookcase or an entryway table.

2. Now, remove all the current items so you can start with a blank canvas. Step back and take inventory of the items. Are there too many? Are there any items that you don't love or that don't fit your personal themes? Anything that really belongs in another room? Set these things aside for now.

3. Next, begin creating your vignette by returning one or two of the items you love. Then walk into other rooms and look for items that would work well in your new vignette. Think textiles, colors, textures, styles, themes, and so on. Just as a stylist does at a professional photo shoot, step back and create a beautiful picture with the items you have chosen. Often, creating beauty is as easy as simplifying or paring down.

4. How did you do? Keep practicing—and remember to play and have fun, too. Take stock of other areas of your home that you may be able to tackle in a few moments. Write this list down in the "Displays of Affection" section of your Dream Diary.

Other ways to play with displays: Plan a party and invite a few close friends who share your decorating muse. Fresh eyes can be a big help and make a project feel less overwhelming. Another fun idea is to invite friends to share cast-off items with one another. A piece that doesn't fit your personal style may become your best friend's newest treasure. However you choose to begin, the more you practice, the better you will become at creating a look you will love to come home to.

7

※·❦·※

PERSONALIZED STYLE

Homes and Styles That Show Individuality

When you are given a nickel tour of a home **that slowly adds up to a dollar** from all the stories behind every piece, **that's style from within.** There is the artist who decorates with her own works of art and even uses her trusty tools as display items. Collectors, decorators, people with a distinct look and taste—even pack rats—all live in homes that are like no other.

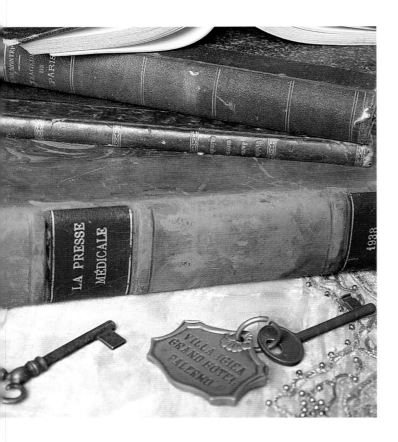

BY NOW, YOU'VE ALREADY BEGUN TO INCORPORATE THIS KIND OF personal vavoom into your own home. Perhaps your great-grandmother's wrought-iron bed, the only belonging she brought when she immigrated to the United States, already reigns in your guest bedroom. Perhaps you found a unique way to display the collection of blue enamel that you hunted everywhere from garage sales to eBay.

ABOVE LEFT: Old French books and keys from an Italian hotel are small keepsakes that display beautifully together, creating an old-world feel.

ABOVE RIGHT: Folds of antique ribbon complement the other collectibles Barbara Cheatley has acquired, reinforcing the rule that if you love something, it will mingle happily with your other pieces.

OPPOSITE: Trinkets such as an enamel locket and a vintage autograph book are especially beautiful when they have a story.

Achieving a home that radiates personalized style begins with confidence. It involves allowing yourself to be inspired by trends but not dependent on them, as no lifelong collector can give up her passion just because it may no longer be in vogue.

Creating personal style is a serendipitous process, so it also requires patience and trust in your own vision. We rarely shop for things in one outing with the idea that they are meant to compose our homes harmoniously. Instead, we acquire the pieces from a variety of places because we feel a connection to each of them. In fact, it is not uncommon to find that two pieces blend wonderfully as if they were intended to be together, such as an antique ribbon and an old locket unified by a blue cornflower, a collection of old hotel keys and French books, or an ink drawing of a moth and a brown leather diary. The joy of discovering how these items play off each other rarely fades.

LEFT: Vintage quilts are rich in craftsmanship and romantic history, which is what influences Barbara Cheatley's love for them. They look especially appealing when stacked in an antique armoire.

OPPOSITE, ABOVE: Three cottage chairs in blue make a dramatic statement against a brick-red wall and blue window frames. One of Barbara's prized finds, the set is missing the fourth chair, which she will forever be on the hunt for.

OPPOSITE, BELOW: Cozy and comfortable, this Adirondack chair displays Barbara's favored treasures perfectly.

FEELING NOSTALGIC

Barbara Cheatley, owner of her eponymous store in Claremont, California, has been collecting since she was a young girl. Drawn to the history of a family treasure, finding romance in the mystery of who once used it, she is especially fond of heirloom pieces, daily souvenirs that connect her to her ancestors. She lives, most appropriately, in an old farmhouse on a former orange grove that has become the ideal showcase for her countless collections.

Cheatley's advice: Consider the reasons why you purchased a piece. Did you have a specific intention or place in mind for it? Or was it something you just had to have? Most likely, the qualities that attracted you to the item share commonalities with other decorative elements you own. Or perhaps you've collected a number of items that remind you of when you were young. Many of us have fond memories of our grandmothers' kitchens, whether of the subway tile backsplash or her earthenware mixing bowls. Chances are you will either be

LEFT: Stumpy pewter mugs are softened with pink roses. The cheerful striped spine of a modern book adds height.

BELOW: Alicia Paulson finds whimsy in childhood figurines, which also add a nostalgic element to a simple bedside setting.

inclined to use the pieces she bestowed on you or you're on a continual quest to find close replicates. That's personality with a special sentimental touch.

Nostalgia may be the decorating trend that, for all the obvious reasons, will never go out of style. The good trends always come back, in part because the designers and style arbiters who dictate them are influenced by the very things they grew up with. Says designer Alicia Paulson, "They happen because people are reimagining a past they are nostalgic for. You like to surround yourself with things, times, and places that were safe and good."

You can easily achieve comfort and feel nurtured when you break out the quilt you used to wrap yourself in while watching *Laverne and Shirley*. And your beloved worn toy animal will always have pride of place in your belongings. Decorate with personality pieces that bring a smile to your face, that connect you to the innocent times of your youth, a safe haven, which is what a home should be.

THEME EVENT

Roosters, daisies, dogs, cats, and all things country barnyard; Staffordshire dogs; Americana; Victorian games—you may even have fallen for a motif at birth, when you were given your first hand-stitched toy lamb that led to a collection you still can't part with. In fact, that stuffed animal may even be the basis of a bedside vignette. We've already covered at length how to use themes to unify opposites and unlike items when you're mixing and matching, but it's also important to note that theme items are a key way to make a place distinctly your own. What better way to pique visitors' interest than with a motif that expresses something personal about you or your family? A dazzling presentation of personal items creates a silent invitation and conversation with guests in your home.

CLOCKWISE FROM TOP LEFT: A cheerful panoply of vintage figural teapots and advertisements dresses this antique possum-belly table embellished with dog head pulls. ● Each of these papier-mâché decorative items from the nineteenth century comes in a range of designs and patterns, which can be punched up with fresh daisies. ● Showcase vintage games and collectibles in den or family room bookshelves to spark conversation among guests. ● Could this home-owner like dogs? Another way to show your passion for something is with sumptuous style and personality. Cover an entire wall with nineteenth-century dog paintings and drawings, as well as favorite photographs of pets past and present. ● These lead play toys of a farm scene can be found in varying conditions at estate sales and antiques stores. The English company Britains makes most of them. ● This comfortable club chair is upholstered in 1940s toile fabric ● Some pieces were inherited; others collected and sought after. Here they come together in a lively corner that connects the passions of this collector.

RIGHT: Blue-and-white porcelain and summer treats create a perfect cottage kitchen.

OPPOSITE: Blue-and-white enamelware was originally used for tea and coffee, created for those who couldn't afford fine china.

COLLECTOR'S PIECE

If you are a born collector but can't seem to feature your obsession in your home, go ahead—display it. Surround yourself with the things you are drawn to, and beauty happens. Like motif and nostalgia pieces, collections share an appealing visual symmetry. The pieces of a collection are like the elements composing a scrapbook. When combined as a group, they provide insight into their owner.

> "You can have collections and live with them, too."

Some collectors imagine their finds can only be used like a precious museum exhibit. But you can have collections and live with them, too. For new collectors, *Romantic Homes* collectibles editor Nancy Ruhling suggests choosing a collectible that enhances everyday life, seeking those objects that are not irreplaceable. For instance, were they mass-produced? Created to be used and sold at reasonable prices, which will therefore be more affordable for today's collector? Or will the pieces endure? Blue enamelware and vintage kitchen tools are perfect examples of beautiful collectibles made to withstand time and use.

doing the polka

How to Create a Polka-Dotted Floor

This is a special technique from Sandy Hall of Good Goods. (See the photograph on page 192.)

1. Cover furniture and the area surrounding the floor with large sheets of plastic or old bed sheets.

2. Begin with a base of white paint (for concrete flooring, use paint made especially for cement). Allow it to dry for 24 hours.

3. Mark the floor according to how you want the dots arranged, either in a straight line or in a pattern. "I like mine in neat little rows," says Sandy Hall. Use a plumb liner string to mark your desired pattern first and then apply painter's tape to seal your pattern, which will help guide you during the painting process.

4. Cut a large sponge into a circle. Use tweezers to make the sponge holes bigger and then attach the sponge to the end of a broomstick by making a hole half the depth of the sponge, placing the broom handle inside, and securing it with Super Glue. Let the glue dry completely.

5. Pour floor paint into a large pan. Dip the surface of the sponge into the paint and blot lightly on a towel.

6. Begin by stamping the dots onto the floor, following your pattern, until the paint wears thin on the sponge. Dip the sponge in the paint, blot, and continue to apply the dots until complete.

7. Allow the dots to dry for 24 hours and then use a roller brush to apply seal to the floor. Sandy recommends four coats of Diamond Finish. Allow the finish to dry according to the manufacturer's directions between coats.

Find beauty in a variety of elements and enhance them in natural light.

TO EACH HER OWN WHIMSY

Just as a metaphorical painting can entrance us with its beauty—no matter how many times you look at it, you can always find something new—homes full of personality are also rich in depth. A great pleasure of decorating is discovering aspects of your style that you weren't previously aware of. Draw inspiration from the homes of others, and their experiments, and conduct your own. Find innovative ways to decorate with everyday things—vintage postcards hung like a mobile by your kitchen window, an arrangement of budding roses

wrapped in kale leaves, or a lace tablecloth used as a window valance. Store up and test-drive those gee-whiz ideas you can't wait to try in your own home, and be prepared for a lot of surprises.

Alicia Paulson is the architect behind the cheerful website rosylittlethings.com. Though her flair for decorating with everything sweet manifests itself in Web pages devoted to handcrafted paper birds, with swatches of baby roses trimming the computer screen, her passion for creating whimsical displays is a recently developed skill. When a

OPPOSITE: It doesn't get more custom-made than pillowcases you embroidered with your initials and favored birds.

RIGHT: You're never too old to outgrow your little bunnies and lambs; in fact, they can become the stars of your bureau.

generous blogger sent Alicia a box of personal treasures including plastic birds and an old locker tag, she marveled at the meaning behind these belongings. "I looked at this pile of things and felt moved by the idea that she gave me this, knowing I would care," says Alicia. Thus she began to carve out spaces in her own home for things that are important to her. "It's a relief to see the prosaic things of your life and have them cataloged."

Alicia creates her home with pure, over-the-top, lollipop fun. She treats it as a canvas, similar to a set designer assigned the task of creating a world with good fairies and talking animals. In her home, guests experience her treatment of combining jolly fabrics with pillowcases adorned with lovebirds she hand-stitched herself. Glazed ceramic kitties and bunnies summon smiles, as does a lamp shade that looks like something a fussy lady would have worn to the voting booth in 1966.

It is no surprise that Alicia styles her home as a fantasy. "It's a farm fantasy," she says, "where I wear cute plaid coats with flower pins and I have stripy wallpaper—everything fits in that imaginary vision."

Farm fantasy, Victorian tea party, or a scene spun from one of Shakespeare's comedies—creating a home from an outlandish theme may be the closest you can come to living out your dream.

GET PERSONAL

Elizabeth Maxson, who calls herself the Queen of Personalization, earns her title from all the unique ways in which she creates a panorama of beauty from a textured variety of vintage items. She even finds design ideas in words and quotes. "I love them," says Maxson. "I have them painted on my walls and on my floor and written on pieces of paper that I hang from the chandeliers—they are everywhere, and I never tire of them." Maxson suggests you think of the maxims you live by and incorporate them into your home.

With the clean geometry of the letters and monochromatic scheme, words are not just inspiring in what they say but also in how they look. Envelopes with your name written on them lend themselves to a punchy collage on a corkboard or a chalkboard. Framing a special letter with extra matting can add interest to a bare wall. Save interesting documents, which may later compose one of your favorite vignettes—a one-of-a-kind way of remaining forever connected to something meaningful.

ABOVE LEFT: Alicia's special things share more of a connection than simply pattern and color.

ABOVE CENTER: Nostalgic keepsakes can be admired when attractively displayed, punching up the starkest of walls.

ABOVE RIGHT: Liberate an untidy box or junk drawer of invitations. When pinned to a corkboard lined with fabric, these little items add style to any corner.

If you love something but don't know how to weave it into your lair, add it to your Vintage Vavoom workbook or start a file or other inspiration book you can refer to. Or, better yet, hang your clippings on an inspiration board, which is often beautiful even as a work in progress. Just punch up a corkboard with a piece of fabric and pinup cards, remnants from a perfect vacation, a ticket from a night that should always be remembered, and you have a visual scrapbook. This is the epitome of living with the past in a modern way.

IMPERFECT BEAUTY

It's the birthmark or gapped teeth that makes a pretty girl beautiful. Imperfection adds character. Maybe the red-handled cookie cutter is in pristine shape, but your heart sings for the green one with chipped paint and a thumb-sized gash. Maybe you have a habit of setting your great-aunt's wobbly table with your anniversary crystal, or of placing your beloved tea-stained mug on a tablecloth you made from a trendy fabric found in the remnants bin.

The subdued colors of shells and pearly Christmas ornaments show that mixing seasonal mainstays achieves one-of-a-kind style.

A painting and a modern vase come together. Add the natural elements of just-blooming roses, and you've completed the look.

ART EXHIBIT

The homes of artists, chock-full of their works, contain some of the most intimate forms of expression. Walls brightened with paintings, cups thrown with the artists' own hands, offer vivid reminders of their style and lifestyle, too. Just as combining the old with the new imparts beauty to both, pairing an artist's creation with other storied pieces gives the work added grandeur.

Don't hesitate to mix new items with old ones, machine-made things with your own crafts; creating a beautiful, timeworn look is not about perfection. Knowing that Vintage Vavoom encourages us to use, not just admire, our found objects, we understand this means they may suffer wear and tear. No matter— imperfections are a reminder that our decorative belongings are not only showpieces but also enhance our quality of life. The Vintage Vavoom philosophy inspires us to relax in a less than perfect environment while surrounded by livable elegance.

Artist Doreen Mellen decorates her home in Laguna Beach, California, with heirlooms and pieces she's acquired through her travels, along with her portraits, ceramics, even works in progress. It's a blend of all the treasures she respects, with an emphasis on one-of-a-kind items that weren't part of a production cycle. These everyday belongings, as well as her works of art, all have meaning and quality, and they are part of a tradition meant to be passed down.

moonlighting

Decorate with pieces that do double duty in your garden:

- Watering cans as flower vases

- Old barrels and salvaged doors as large tables

- Broken china or pots for garden borders to add color and whimsy

- Old rakes from which to hang gardening tools or other accessories

- Lobster cages as small tables

- Christmas tree lights for soft lighting framing a window year-round

- The wicker basket of a showpiece bicycle to display your prized roses

- Vintage signs to add points of interest

MAKE IT YOURS

Some of the most personal homes include pieces the dweller made herself. Though not everyone has the skills to embroider her own pillows, almost anyone can paste wallpaper remnants and initials on an envelope, or repurpose soup cans by gluing vintage paper and ribbon on them and hanging them on a chandelier.

If you are a big tea drinker and find that you have accumulated a surplus of teacups through-out the years but do not have the heart to part with them, weave the handles through sturdy sailing rope and drape them around a banister. Save the ribbon streamers from an old theme party and pitch them along your garden for an effect as grand as sounding trumpets in a royal court. Those are special small touches that are close to the heart and rich in the retelling.

REGROUP AND REFURBISH

Old pieces can be given a fresh look when paired with trendier items. Having trouble sourcing that perfect addition you have in your mind? Manipulate an antique or weather a newer piece. "I love doing this," says Elizabeth Maxson. "I have a round cherrywood dining room table dating from about 1900, which I painted and surrounded by new chairs that I painted in the same shade."

OPPOSITE AND ABOVE LEFT: Teacups hung on a rope and colorful flags welcome guests to Old Tustin, California's McCharles House tea room, beckoning them inside.

LEFT AND TOP RIGHT: Here's an easy way to feature garden clippings with originality and style: Recycle a basic tin can, adorn it with vintage clip art, and embellish it with colored ribbons and your favorite flowers to create a one-of-a-kind vessel that adds drama to your home.

GET FLOORED

We commonly consider our eye-level surroundings as the ultimate stages for our displays; however, the floors we stand on can be
one of the best places to add drama. An ordinary wood floor is gussied up when painted
with such classical patterns as hexagons and
colorful borders. Choose a color and pattern
you love and hire a contractor. Or, for DIYers,
try it yourself. Barbara Cheatley created her
floor, which suitably matches her collection of
nineteenth-century papier-mâché daisy pieces
and Staffordshire. Her original floor was in
such poor condition it had to be replaced.
Barbara then painted over the new floor in a
black-and-white geometric pattern and mod-
eled the border from a Laura Ashley print.

In Sandy Hall's store, Good Goods, in Visalia,
California, the blue polka-dot floor always
elicits coos and inquiries from visitors. What's
even more enticing is that Sandy did it herself,
and it can be easily replicated. Vavoom doesn't
get more personal than a blue-spotted floor
you created on your own. (See page 182 for
instructions.)

OPPOSITE: Personalize your space with a favorite decorative element, such as this blue polka-dot floor.
THIS PAGE, CLOCKWISE FROM TOP LEFT: Vintage touches that all come with a story bring an inviting look to this sun-drenched conservatory. ● A variety of collectibles receive their proper due when the focus is on quality, color, and theme. ● A hand-painted checked floor adds drama to a special room. ● The look of distressed wood, even on the most banal of objects, adds a vintage appeal. ● Cute and stylish, animal figurines enhance a tabletop tableau.

GARDEN VARIETY

Just as the beauty of a home is enhanced by flowers and elements culled from the outdoors, your
garden can also draw on the bounties intended for
inside your house. Take a nod from the Arts and
Crafts movement, which emphasized the value in
blurring the lines between indoors and out. To
seize the healthy benefits of the outdoors, think of
your garden, yard, patio, and deck as extensions of
your home décor. Though the grand space can be
intimidating, lacking the precise, squared measure-
ments of a floor plan, let the landscape direct
you—anything without flowers is free territory in
which to develop your romantic space.

Some of the most romantic gardens feature
unexpected touches, as whimsical as poles with
ribbons or a mermaid sign announcing the house
number—appropriately located on Mermaid
Street.

Freshen outdoor furniture with a coat of
paint and then bring your tableware outside
for a meal alfresco. Even old jam jars can be
used as vessels for your cuttings, and you
won't be so hard-pressed to tidy up, as they
can weather the elements.

In a private space, usually under the canopy
of an old tree, create a hidden, inviting nook.
This is the perfect opportunity to put those
vintage purchases to use! Architectural salvage,
such as an old chandelier lit with candles and
a stained-glass window frame, adds grandeur

and romance in an enchanting spot boxed in with invisible walls. Imagination is key to creating a personalized outdoors space, where old tubs become planters and a wrought-iron bed can be used for late afternoon naps or to delineate a part of your garden.

Also consider your natural palette, finding inspiration in sunlight, the surrounding flower beds, and the tone of the late afternoon sky. You may be surprised by how perfectly your everyday things blend with such outdoor ele-

ments as sheer draperies playing off the sun and colorful Fiestaware that complements a patch of tiger lilies.

Add a modern flair by covering a picnic table with a few yards of the latest sumptuous fabric and tossing a few coordinating pillows on chairs. Then mix it up with a Vintage Vavoom display of artfully arranged garden tools, glass bottles, or retro serving pieces on the main table and a classic apron or dish towel placed on a side table.

Personalized Style
DREAM DIARY WORKSHOP:
SHOW YOUR INDIVIDUALITY

Find out where you are today—and where you want to go!

1. Review what you've learned from your favorites map and personal themes list. Then take an assessment of your home today. Write the name of each room at the top of a blank piece of paper. A clipboard can make the next step easier.

    Stand in each room and observe whether the themes you've learned throughout this book are coming through. Are there items you have held onto but don't love? Are there personal themes you haven't expressed in any of your rooms? Some major room renovation you think about every time you walk into this room? Does a favorite piece of furniture seem hidden? Can you identify double-duty items that can be used in another way? Are there pieces of furniture or accessories that should be moved to another room? Jot it all down.

    Whenever you can, list items that are obvious candidates for you to donate to charity or give away to a friend. It's not as hard to let go of belongings when you know that someone else will enjoy them more. Besides, in being selective, you're making space for Vintage Vavoom that will be closer to your heart and that will better fill your home with your personality.

2. Take each room list and break it down into a task list by category, from easiest to most difficult:

    - *To give away or donate*
    - *To put away temporarily (rotate vignette items from your prop closet or other storage) or rearrange*
    - *To purchase (or plan to acquire) in order to express more items in a favorite theme*
    - *To use or purchase for future renovation or décor update (paint, window treatments, etc.)*

3. Mark dates on your calendar and set deadlines to complete the tasks for each room. Begin with the simpler tasks. Schedule one room at a time, starting with giving away or donating items to create more space to show off what's really expressive of you. File the room lists under each corresponding heading in your binder.

8

BASICS
OF CARE

Maintaining Your Fineries

Serious collectors with important pieces must safeguard their items. Nancy Ruhling, who contributes to *Romantic Homes*'s collectibles column, reminds us that hazards to treasured pieces can be found everywhere. "Sunlight, dust, heat, air conditioning—even the touch of an ungloved hand will compromise antiques," she says.

TEXTILE MESSAGES

Safe care of our finest linens is as involved and detailed as the history and stories behind them. They were created lovingly, meant to be passed down and enjoyed by future generations. Maintaining their condition means showing them the respect they deserve.

Storage

As antique dinnerware was created to be used, so were linens. Use and enjoy your finest textiles; showcase them to add beauty to your home while enjoying the wonder they evoke. In fact, long-term storage can be detrimental to your linens, resulting in yellowing and rendering them more prone to damage from harmful temperatures, moths, and rodents. Considering that limited storage is inevitable in a romantic home (yes, we know you love to accumulate things and hate to part with them!), store your finer textiles properly to maintain their strength.

TAKE THE NECESSARY PRECAUTIONS WITH YOUR VALUED ITEMS by displaying them in glass cases in temperature-controlled rooms. "And don't ever dust them," warns Ruhling. "Cleaning can harm the patina and texture and greatly decrease the value."

ABOVE: When this laundry bag was created, the initials helped family members identify their washables. In the present, it adds beauty and function to a treasured home.

OPPOSITE: Sturdy heirloom linens always please the eye, especially when punched up with a special piece, such as this embroidered laundry bag.

DECORATIVE
CLEANING
PRODUCTS

Antique cleaning products and paraphernalia are fantastic decorative items with plenty of their own Vintage Vavoom. Soapboxes, laundry bags, jars of wooden clothespins, vinegar bottles, enamel buckets, washboards, and notions kits—line them on an open shelf, and you have a wonderful display. They are also visual reminders of the safe, trusted cleaning methods we should employ.

Considering that those antique laundry bags had initials sewed in for identification purposes, you are living history if each member of the family uses an assigned laundry basket to keep things tidy. You'll also increase the likelihood that clothes will be deposited in a bag, not on the floor.

An enamel bucket does double duty as a vase for flowers.

safe storage

Tips for long-term care of linens:

🦋 Begin by choosing a suitable space that maintains a room temperature of between 68 and 77 degrees Fahrenheit. While attics and basements are tempting storage spots, they often subject items to harmful erratic temperatures, extreme heat, and dank mildew. Designate a closet specifically for the storage of your finer things, or carve out a space beneath your bed.

🦋 Wash items before storing them so as not to attract pests; however, do not dry clean, as those harmful chemicals can damage your treasures. For the proper cleaning technique, see page 207.

🦋 Be careful not to fold your linens. Creases cause yellowing and weaken fibers. Either roll them or bunch them in a soft ball.

🦋 Pack linens in acid-free tissue, as ordinary paper and cardboard cause fabrics to deteriorate.

🦋 Store with cedar chips—which are more pleasing to the scenses than nosehair-singeing moth-balls—to inhibit moths. Add lavender sachets or sheets of fabric softener to keep your linens freshly scented.

Properly caring for timeworn pieces helps keep beautiful heirlooms to be passed down.

A CLEAN HISTORY

As your most cherished items have beautifully endured the test of time, treat them in the centuries-old manner they were accustomed to. Like any fine skill, the arts of laundering, mending, and home maintenance can be learned from our ancestors. First, if you read the labels of some of those touted miracle cleaners stowed beneath the kitchen sink, a skull and crossbones would seem more appropriate branding than the cheery colors and animated bubbles that say "buy me." To treat our finest belongings with such toxic chemicals, not to mention putting ourselves into contact with these hazardous ingredients, is inviting harm into our homes.

NATURALLY SPEAKING

In *Romantic Homes*'s "Healthy Home" column, we address the importance of using natural cleansers and materials—and, naturally, the benefits are plentiful. Our possessions look

better and last longer; the ingredients are safe and usually inexpensive. Most important, we can trust in the air we breathe. Consider and reexamine every household product you're in contact with. Even an innocent-looking sponge is a toxic breeding ground for bacteria. Put old sponges in the microwave for two minutes or routinely toss them. Choose natural cleansing ingredients such as white vinegar, lemons, and baking soda over chemically charged detergents, notably toilet bowl cleaners and waxes. Instead of turning on the air conditioning, get in the habit of keeping the windows open, which ventilates and removes harmful chemicals from your home. Even the candles we use can invite trouble; choose soy-based or paraffin candles so your air stays natural and fresh.

> "As your most cherished items have beautifully endured the test of time, treat them in the centuries-old manner they were accustomed to."

WASHING CARE

How you wash vintage textiles depends on each fabric. Avoid dry cleaning, harmful bleach, starches, and the dryer. White vinegar and baking soda are excellent natural bleaches, while clear soap, lemon juice, rubbing alcohol, seltzer, and even plain water can all be used to remove fresh stains from sturdy cotton.

Fine items, such as heirloom pieces, linens, and those tablecloths and handkerchiefs that have the lacy patterns of spun sugar, we recommend you wash by hand. Fill a large round bucket or a deep sink with a natural, gentle detergent made specifically for delicates. Follow the package instructions carefully. Swish each item separately, rinse well until all the soap is removed, and wrap gently in a towel, which is safer than the manic spin cycle. Never wring! Lay your items flat on a towel to dry. Be vigilant when drying your finest linens outdoors, as the sun can be a wonderful natural bleach but also fades and wears fabrics. Your linen luxuries are also susceptible to outdoor elements such as dirt and animals.

Look to your favored buttons not only as mending essentials but also as decorative features in your home.

Antique linens and fine upholstery can be enjoyed and used every day with thoughtful attention to care.

MENDING AND PRESSING

You can mend vintage textiles to strengthen weak areas and use beautiful fabric remnants, buttons, and ribbons to give worn items a new life. Be sure to wash the items before repairing them, as shrinkage can occur. Press items with a low steam heat, using a pressing cloth atop fragile fabrics such as silk organza. Test a small, hidden section of the fabric before getting started. Plain flour-sack dish towels or clean white pieces of cotton, recycled from worn sheets, make wonderful pressing cloths. In fact, a clean, retired sheet placed on the floor around the ironing board keeps large items like tablecloths dirt-free. Repurposed old bedsheets, curtains, even clothes, can also be used for your sewing and mending projects. Always have the right tools on hand, such as fine linen thread, a variety of needles, and shears reserved for use on fabrics. If you are all thumbs when it comes to a needle and thread, enlist a trusted tailor. To find a good tailor, get referrals from an antiques dealer or store owner who specializes in antique linens. Also, research historic house museums in your area. The antique textile docent can be a great resource for tips, too.

Basics of Care
DREAM DIARY WORKSHOP: PROPER CARE FOR YOUR FINE THINGS

Do you have fine silver that needs to be polished? Jewelry that needs fixing? A favorite figurine that needs to be repaired so it can be displayed?

Keep an ongoing list, as well as a list of experts you can hire to help with more difficult jobs like restoring a painting or mending antique lace, for example. Always ask for referrals. And when you find information in magazines or news clippings to help you do it yourself, three-hole-punch and file them in the "Basics of Care" section of your binder for future reference.

PUBLIC

INDEPENDENCE, OREGON
                                    aug 27 1947
ng hops   pickers registered for you and
              knowing if there are any changes.
ation is for the farms circled below and YOUR
ULD BE SO ADDRESSED
          (Hanna Ranch)   W. H. Walker Ranch
aged   DEAN WALKER FARMS   Farm
                              ___ E Hood

CONCLUSION

Vintage Vavoom is more than just a nostalgic nod to the past.

It is a wonderful excuse to surround yourself with the things you love every day, and an invitation to your visitors to get to know you better. It is a way of making your home both beautiful and livable, because you recognize that imperfections are a sign of character and individuality, that a chipped plate holds warm memories of dinner parties with beloved friends, or the pure delight of being given a slice of freshly baked pie after dinner as a child.

Vintage Vavoom comes not only with a sense of history but also with a sense of humor. As you've now seen, you can explore your passions and joys through your collections, displays, and purchases—there's no reason not to decorate with your favorite things, from heirloom timepieces to perfect pink-sprinkled cupcakes. It is our hope that reading this book, filling out your Dream Diary Workshops, foraging among the things that you already own, and taking shopping trips have opened your eyes to all the treasures just waiting to be part of your own Vintage Vavoom home.

Jacqueline deMontravel, Hillary Black, Shelley Baugh, Rebecca Razo, and Merrie Destefano, the editors of *Romantic Homes*

RESOURCES

SHOPPING

Anthropologie
www.anthropologie.com

**Antique European Linens
and Decadence Down**
www.antiqueeuropeanlinens.com

Barbara Cheatley's
Claremont, California
(909) 621-4161

Blanc d'Ivoire
www.blancdivoire.com

Blue & White Porcelain
www.blue-white-porcelain.com

Bountiful
Venice, California
(310) 450-3620
www.bountifulhome.com

Bungalow
Laguna Beach, California
(949) 494-0191
www.bungalowfurnishings.com

Calico Corners
(800) 213-6366
www.calicocorners.com

The Cat's Meow
Venice, Florida
(941) 486-1650
www.catsmeowinc.com

The Chandler Collection
(800) 258-2229
www.thechandlercollection.com

The Chartreuse Pear
Ruston, Louisiana
(318) 255-7327

Chez M'Lain
www.chezmlain.com

Dash & Albert
www.dashandalbert.com

Doreen Mellen, Artist
Laguna Beach, California
(949) 510-7935

Elizabeth House
Maplewood, Missouri
(314) 644-0828
www.elizabethhouse.us

Enchanted Treasures
Fairhaven, Massachusetts
(866) 990-8444
www.enchantedtreasures.com

Florilegium
Parkville, Missouri
(816) 746-6164
www.florilegium.com

Free Spirit Fabric
www.freespiritfabric.com

French General
Hollywood, California
(323) 462-0818
www.frenchgeneral.com

Funktion Home
www.funktionhome.com

Good Goods
Visalia, California
(559) 594-5765

The Grand Emporium
San Pedro, California
(310) 514-8429

**Klaradal Swedish Antiques
and Furnishings**
Olney, Maryland
(301) 570-2557
www.klaradal.com

Limoges Antiques Shop
Andover, Massachusetts
(978) 470-8773
www.limogesantiques.com

Match, Inc.
(201) 792-9444
www.match1995.com

McCharles House
Tustin, California
(714) 731-4063
www.mccharleshouse.com

MiLady's Linens
Gardiner, Maine
(207) 582-3033

The Monogram Shop
East Hampton, New York
(631) 329-3379
www.themonogramshops.com

Muff's Hardware
Orange, California
(714) 997-0243
www.muffshardware.com

Pom Pom
Los Angeles, California
(323) 938-6286
www.pompominteriors.com

P.O.S.H. Chicago
Chicago, Illinois
(312) 280-1602
www.poshchicago.com

Potluck Studios
(800) 559-7341
www.potluckstudios.com

Quel Objet
(877) 762-4499
www.quelobjet.com

Rosanna, Inc.
www.rosannainc.com

Sandra Evertson
Paris Flea Market Design
www.fleamarketdesigns.com

Sharyn Blond Linens
(913) 362-4420
www.sharynblondlinens.com

Vervain
(800) 611-8686
www.vervain.com

The Village House
(800) 694-8602
www.villagehouse.net

Vintage Weave
Los Angeles, California
(323) 932-0451
www.vintageweave.com

Watson Kennedy
Seattle, Washington
(800) 991-9361
www.watsonkennedy.com

Wesley Allen
Los Angeles, California
(877) 893-2337
http://rh.wesleyallen.com

NOTED FLEA MARKETS

Alameda Point Antiques and Collectibles Fair
Alameda, California
(800) 982-9822
www.antiquesbythebay.net or
www.auctionsbythebay.com

Annex/Hell's Kitchen Flea Market
New York, New York
(212) 243-5343
www.annexmarkets.com

Brimfield Antiques Show
Brimfield, Massachusetts
www.brimfieldshow.com

Elephant's Trunk Country Flea Market
New Milford, Connecticut
(508) 896-1975
www.etflea.com

Flamingo Promotions
From Manhattan to Maine
(631) 261-4590
www.flamingoshow.com

Kane County Flea Market
St. Charles, Illinois
(630) 377-2252
www.kanecountyfleamarket.com

Lakewood Antiques Market
Atlanta, Georgia
(770) 889-3400
www.lakewoodantiques.com

Lakewood 400 Antiques Fair
Cumming, Georgia
(404) 622-4488 or (770) 889-3400
www.lakewoodantiques.com

Monticello Antique Marketplace
Portland, Oregon
(503) 256-8600
www.monticelloantiques.com

Rose Bowl Flea Market
Pasadena, California
(323) 560-7469
www.rgsshows.com

Showplace Antique Center
New York, New York
(212) 633-6063
www.nyshowplace.com

ACKNOWLEDGMENTS

We would like to acknowledge all the homeowners, shopkeepers, and contributing photographers and stylists without whom this book would not have been created. We are grateful for the graciousness of those who opened their doors and granted us leave to move furniture and inspect cabinets and allowed us the freedom to make magic happen. Their remarkable creativity is captured on each page.

Thanks to *Romantic Homes* contributing editors Elizabeth Maxson, Carolyn Westbrook, and Nancy Ruhling, whose knowledge we hold in great esteem; to Aliza Fogelson, our editor, who certainly has Vintage Vavoom; and to our ace agent, Eleanor Jackson, whose style, intelligence, and talent are a constant inspiration.

PHOTOGRAPHERS

Kindra Clineff, Wanelle Fitch, Jaimee Itagaki, Chris Little, Vince Lupo, Rusty Reniers, Matthew Roharik, Franklin and Esther Schmidt, Michael Skott, Mark Tanner, and Jessie Walker

HOMEOWNERS

Shelley and Jay Baugh, Susie and Ed Beall, Jodi Califano, Nancy Cassity, Barbara Cheatley, Becky Clark, Jeanette Donaher, Nancy Feldman, Marylyn Ginsburg, Amanda Heer, Vivian and Audrey Heredia, Michelle and Bob Hipolito, Susie and Mark Holt, Karen and John Kennedy, Sue and Peter Kopperman, Melissa Ladaire, Roberta Laprade, Brenda and Richard Lee, Larry and Melissa Lewis, Michael Lindsay, Marsha Manchester, Doreen and Brian Mellen, Rebecca and Steve Nelson, Albert Nichols, Alicia and Andy Paulson, Rita Razo, Marcia Sola, Sue and Rick Sparks, John and Gay Van Beek, Pat Whalen

INDEX